BAKER'S*

BEST *Chocolate*

COOKBOOK

BRIMAR

© 1995 Brimar Publishing Inc.
338 Saint Antoine St. East
Montreal, Quebec, Canada H2Y 1A3
Tel: (514) 954-1441
Fax: (514) 954-5086

Photography: Nathalie Dumouchel
Food Preparation/Stylist: Josée Robitaille
Assistant Stylist: Louis Hudon
Graphic Design: Zapp
Props courtesy of: Arthur Quentin
Stokes
Pier 1 Imports
Les Carreaux Ramca Ltd.

Pictured on the front cover:
BAKER'S Best Celebration Cake *(see recipe, page 95)*

BAKER'S, ANGEL FLAKE, KRAFT, COOL WHIP, JELL-O, MAGIC MOMENTS, MIRACLE WHIP, PHILADELPHIA BRAND and the "LA BELLE CHOCOLATIÈRE" design are registered Trade-Marks of Kraft Canada Inc.

BAKER'S KITCHENS is a Trade-Mark of Kraft Canada Inc.

Acknowledgments:

Among the many people who helped to produce this book, we would like to especially acknowledge Cécile Girard-Hicks, Director BAKER'S KITCHENS and her enthusiastic staff of food professionals including: Marilynn Small, Marian Macdonald, Judy Welden, Jane Carman, Susanne Stark, Olga Kaminskyj, Monica Beaumont, Cathy Edwards, Karen German, Maxine Karpel, Barb Martyn, Karen Massari and Michele McAdoo.

Questions? Call the BAKER'S Hotline. Your call will be answered by an experienced food professional - one of the helpful staff in the BAKER'S KITCHENS.

The BAKER'S Hotline is open Monday to Friday 9:00 a.m. until 4:00 p.m. (E.S.T.). Any questions or comments, please feel free to call 1-800-268-6450.

Canadian Cataloguing in Publication Data
Main entry under title:
Baker's Best chocolate cookbook

Issued also in French under title:
Baker's : le chocolat à son meilleur.
Includes index.
ISBN 2-89433-177-0

1. Cookery (Chocolate) I. Title: Best chocolate cookbook.

TX767.C5B35 1995 641.6'374 C95-900317-7

Printed in Canada

BAKER'S
C BEST *hocolate*
COOKBOOK

CHOCOLATE . . . . the very word conjures up luscious fantasies and memories of mouth-watering delights. The welcoming chocolate brownies and milk Mom set out as an after school treat. The fabulous fudge cake that appeared, flaming with candles, on family birthdays. Summer afternoons on Grandma's porch, with freshly baked chocolate cookies and lemonade. Heavenly chocolate sauce dripping down your favourite ice cream. Melt-in-your-mouth chocolate cheesecake.

BAKER'S Chocolate has always been part of those delicious memories. For over 200 years we have been producing chocolate, the fine rich, pure baking chocolate that makes those memorable desserts. Today, in the tradition of bringing you the finest quality chocolate products, the Home Economists in the BAKER'S KITCHENS take pride and pleasure in presenting over 125 of our very best chocolate recipes. This recipe collection should satisfy even the most insatiable cravings including all those special recipes you remember, treasured old world classics, family favourites, plus some tempting new creations with the most popular of all ingredients . . . . CHOCOLATE.

The recipes reflect our correspondence and conversations on our 1-800 lines with thousands of consumers. This is a collection of our most requested recipes. In a very real sense, every consumer who has ever called or written has had a hand in this cookbook's planning. We have provided you with our "Tricks of the Trade" to share with you some of the discoveries that we have made over the years, that will make your baking experiences most enjoyable and successful.

Each of these recipes has been carefully triple-tested in the BAKER'S KITCHENS to taste and look great, so you can be assured that they will work perfectly for you. In some cases step-by-step photos are provided for additional assistance.

Throughout the book we've indicated the recipes that we consider to be *Extra Easy*. These recipes require limited equipment, little time or experience. They are perfect for beginner bakers, kids or experienced bakers who want fast, easy results.

We hope that the recipes in this book will add to the joy you bring to your family and friends.

BAKER'S KITCHENS

CONTENTS

LOOKING BACK:
The History of BAKER'S Chocolate

The story of chocolate goes back to the discovery of the New World. Among the treasures Columbus brought back to King Ferdinand were a few cocoa beans. No one knew what to do with them until later when Cortez visited Mexico. There in the court of Montezuma he drank a brew made from these mysterious beans. The Aztecs called it "cachuatl" meaning "gift from the gods". Cortez brought the chocolate back to Spain and eventually the drink was introduced to the rest of Europe. Soon chocolate houses appeared everywhere, and stopping at one to sip the delicious hot drink and catch up on gossip became part of the social routine.

THE ROMANCE OF "LA BELLE CHOCOLATIÈRE"

The girl whose profile graces every square of BAKER'S Chocolate worked in such a chocolate house in Vienna. Her name was Babette Baldauf.

One day, in 1760, a team of four Lippizaner horses drew up before the chocolate shop with the young Prince Dietrichstein. He sat down at a table and ordered a cup of chocolate, and as he savoured his drink, his eyes never left Babette. He came back to Babette every afternoon for another cup, until finally, the Prince asked Babette if she would consider preparing his chocolate every day for the rest of his life.

As an engagement present, the Prince commissioned Jean Etienne Liotard, a Swiss painter, to paint a portrait of Babette as he had first seen her in her chocolate shop uniform. The artist entitled his painting "La Belle Chocolatière".

Two generations later, Walter Baker discovered "La Belle Chocolatière" hanging in the Dresden Museum. As soon as he heard the romantic story of Babette and the Prince, he immediately adopted the portrait as the trademark of the family company started by his grandfather in 1780.

"La Belle Chocolatière" stamp on each square of BAKER'S Chocolate is a reminder of BAKER'S high quality standards started in 1780 and which continue today with BAKER'S 100% pure, quality chocolate.

HOW CHOCOLATE IS MADE

BAKER'S seeks out the best cocoa bean crops every year and carefully blends many varieties to achieve that deep, rich flavour that chocolate lovers prize. After roasting at high temperatures to develop the chocolate flavour, the cocoa beans are shelled and the remaining nibs are crushed into a thick liquid called chocolate liquor, containing only the chocolate solids and the rich and creamy cocoa butter.

All of the BAKER'S family of fine chocolate products starts with real, pure chocolate liquor. BAKER'S makes a variety of chocolates for use in all your favourite chocolate baking and desserts. There is:

BAKER'S Unsweetened Chocolate, solid chocolate liquor with nothing added.

◆

BAKER'S Semi-Sweet Chocolate, containing chocolate liquor plus additional cocoa butter and sugar.

◆

BAKER'S Bittersweet Chocolate, containing chocolate liquor, additional cocoa butter and sugar but with a darker more pronounced European chocolate flavour, due to the higher chocolate liquor content.

◆

BAKER'S Sweet Chocolate is rich and creamy with a milder chocolate flavour and still more cocoa butter and sugar – exactly as it was in 1852, when the formula was developed.

◆

BAKER'S White Chocolate is made with cocoa butter, milk and sugar, without the cocoa solids, making it creamy white in colour and mild and sweet in flavour.

◆

BAKER'S Chocolate Chips in Semi-Sweet, White, Milk Chocolate, and Butterscotch are made especially to hold their shape in cookies, bars and muffins, even as they soften during baking.

Remember, never substitute one chocolate for another in a recipe as this will affect the flavour and may cause the dessert to fail. For best results do not substitute chocolate chips for BAKER'S Chocolate Squares. BAKER'S squares are specially formulated with quality ingredients to melt easier and smoother than chocolate chips.

WORKING WITH CHOCOLATE
THE TRICKS OF THE TRADE

Storing Chocolate

Keep chocolate in a cool place, below 75°F (24°C) if possible. At high temperatures, chocolate grays in colour (called "blooming") indicating that cocoa butter has merely risen to the surface. Change of colour, however, does not impair flavour or quality. The "bloom" will disappear upon melting.

Melting Chocolate

Chocolate must be handled with care and the melting must be done very gently as chocolate may scorch or burn. Keep in mind that chocolate held in the hands melts quite readily so there's no need for a lot of heat.

The BAKER'S Kitchens recommend two ways to melt BAKER'S Chocolate Squares for general baking (i.e. cake batter, brownies), the **Hot Water Method or** the **Microwave Method**.

Hot Water Method: An easy, no-fail method that requires little equipment.
To melt chocolate squares, unwrap chocolate and chop each square into 8 pieces. Place the chopped chocolate in a small bowl. Set the bowl over another bowl that contains **hot** tap water. Stir until the chocolate is melted. The water may need to be changed if you are melting several squares. It is not necessary to use a double boiler on the stove; water from the tap is hot enough.

Microwave Method: To melt chocolate squares in the microwave, unwrap squares, chop and place in a microwaveable bowl. Melt on MEDIUM power for 2 to 3 minutes for two squares, stirring once. Increase time for more chocolate. Watch carefully, microwave ovens vary. Do not overheat.
Note: Do not let any water drip into the chocolate – a single drop will cause the chocolate to tighten (seize), making it stiff and impossible to work with. If this happens, stir in 1 tsp (5 mL) vegetable oil or shortening for each square of chocolate. Do not use butter or margarine as they contain water and will make the problem worse. Some recipes call for chocolate to be melted with liquids. It is a matter of proportions: a lot of liquid will not tighten the chocolate, but a little will.

Partially Melting Technique (for Plain Glazes, Solid Coatings, Drizzling, Free-form Shapes, Cut-outs, Leaves, and Dipping)

Partially Melting is the technique used for ANYTHING WHERE THE CHOCO-LATE MUST BE FIRST MELTED AND RESET IN A DIFFERENT FORM i.e. dipping fruit or truffles, bark, homemade candies or making chocolate decorations such as drizzles or leaves. This technique has been specially developed in the BAKER'S KITCHENS to **ensure the chocolate will stay hard at room temperature and have a rich, dark, glossy finish.**

1. Chop each square into 8 pieces each and place them in a bowl over **hot** tap water – not boiling water. (Do not use a microwave oven for this – it is too easy to overheat).

2. Melt, stirring constantly, until the point where about one-third of the chocolate is still unmelted.

   Note: The small pieces of solid chocolate will help stabilize the melted portion, to make the chocolate set firm and glossy and to ensure that it stays that way when you serve it.

3. Remove the bowl from over the water and continue stirring until completely smooth. Be patient, it will eventually all melt. The chocolate should feel lukewarm (about 87°F or 30°C).

Always use *partially melted* chocolate while it's still lukewarm. If you're using it for dipping truffles or fruit, set the chocolate over a pan of lukewarm water to keep it from cooling down too quickly. Refrigerate (do not freeze) to set the chocolate quickly – if it cools down too slowly, the chocolate may have streaks on it.

A cool room is the best place for this kind of work with *partially melted* chocolate. The ideal temperature is 60°F or 16°C. The cool room will set the chocolate quickly with no need for refrigeration. If the room temperature is higher, refrigerate to set.

CHOCOLATE GARNISHING TECHNIQUES

BAKER'S Chocolate is not only rich and delicious inside everyone's favourite dessert, it's also beautiful to look at. A chocolate rose leaf, a birthday initial, a festive drizzle pattern, the perfect chocolate curl are all just waiting to be created from a BAKER'S chocolate square.

Indulge your fancy. Give your creative instincts full rein with chocolate – the process is so easy to master and the results so rewarding!

Chocolate Curls

Remember to warm the chocolate slightly until the texture is pliable enough to curl by:

- microwaving on defrost for approximately 1 minute per square or
- hold the wrapped chocolate square in the palm of your hand until chocolate softens slightly.

When chocolate is slightly softened and pliable, carefully draw a vegetable peeler over the smooth surfaces of the square, the bottom for long curls, the sides for short ones. Use a toothpick to lift the curls without breaking them. Sprinkle with icing sugar for a special effect. While the chocolate is the right texture, peel off extra curls to keep in the refrigerator for:

- decorating a cake
- piling on a cheesecake
- dressing up ice cream
- or making any dessert extra special.

Grating

Use a fine or coarse grater. For larger pieces, use a coarse grater and warm the chocolate as you would for chocolate curls. Grate chocolate onto a piece of waxed paper. While you're at it, grate some extra chocolate to keep on hand for:

- folding into any plain cake batter for a flecked effect and subtle chocolate flavour
- garnishing glazed cookies
- dusting over a frosted cake
- covering candies
- decorating chocolate mousse.

Drizzling

Partially melt chocolate with 1 tsp (5 mL) oil over hot water. The oil makes the chocolate less firm when set – therefore easier to cut. Remove from heat and continue stirring until completely melted. Drizzle chocolate with a spoon, or use the plastic bag drizzling technique (pour chocolate into a small plastic bag; poke a small hole with a toothpick into the end of the bag; squeeze out chocolate). For a feathered effect, drizzle in evenly spaced lines over icing and draw a knife across the chocolate lines. Refrigerate to set chocolate.

Glazing

For a plain chocolate glaze with no additions, *partially melt* the chocolate over hot water. Remove from heat and continue stirring until completely melted. Spread over dessert immediately. Tap the pan on the counter to distribute the glaze smoothly, or zigzag a knife through the chocolate to create your own pattern on:
◆ brownies
◆ squares
◆ a plain cake.
Then refrigerate to set chocolate.

Freeform Shapes

Partially melt chocolate over hot water. Remove from heat and continue stirring until completely melted.
Make your own decorating cone from waxed paper, or use a small plastic bag, with a tiny opening cut in one corner on the sealed end. Pour melted chocolate into decorating tube and pipe into desired shapes over waxed paper. You can slide a homemade stencil under the waxed paper as a guide or work freeform. Fill in with chocolate, or use just the outline. Chill. Carefully remove chocolate from waxed paper. Store in refrigerator. Create:
◆ numbers and initials for birthday cakes
◆ whimsical butterflies to top a mousse
◆ line drawings (profiles, caricatures, cartoon characters)

Chocolate Cut-outs

Partially melt chocolate over hot water. Remove from heat and continue stirring until completely melted. Pour onto a waxed paper-lined baking sheet. Cover with another sheet of waxed paper and roll lightly with a rolling pin until 1/8 inch (.3 cm) thick. Chill until set, about 5 minutes. Peel off top layer of waxed paper and cut shapes with cookie cutters or paper patterns. (If you find the chocolate too brittle to cut, let stand at room temperature for a few minutes). Save any remaining pieces of chocolate for melting down and reusing later. Store decorations in refrigerator. Here are just a few ideas to make:

◆ sun, moon and stars for a space-themed cake
◆ "wafers" and butterflies for ice cream
◆ hearts and flowers for Valentine's desserts
◆ bells and Santas for holiday treats

Chocolate Leaves

Partially melt chocolate over hot water. Remove from heat and continue stirring until completely melted. With a small brush, small metal spatula or small spoon, carefully coat the underside of a fresh leaf (do not use poisonous leaves such as philodendron, poinsettia etc.) that doesn't have any fine hairs on it. Rose, maple – even cabbage will do! The chocolate layer should be about 1/16 inch (.2 cm) thick. Be careful not to get any chocolate on the front side of the leaf, or you won't be able to remove it easily.

Put the leaf, chocolate side up, on a waxed paper-lined baking sheet. For a curled leaf effect, cut a paper towel roll in half lengthwise and set leaves inside. Chill until set, about 15 minutes. Hold leaf by the stem to peel off the chocolate. Store in refrigerator until ready to arrange on:

◆ an elegant torte
◆ a chocolate cheesecake
◆ a chocolate pie

Dipping

Partially melt chocolate over hot water. Remove from heat and continue stirring until completely melted. To keep the chocolate at the proper temperature for dipping, set the chocolate over another pan of lukewarm water, about 88°F (30°C). Work quickly making sure the melted chocolate maintains an even, warm temperature. Stir the chocolate during dipping to maintain an even temperature throughout to assure rich, glossy coating. For dipping, the type of chocolate used and the correct temperature are the two most important factors for success. Work in a cool place; chill the dipped chocolates quickly.

To dip fruits, wash and dry thoroughly on paper towel. Dip half of fruit into chocolate. Place on waxed paper-lined baking sheet. Chill until set. Store in refrigerator.

To dip candied fruits and nuts, hold using fingertips for partial dipping or completely cover with melted chocolate and remove with fork. Place on waxed paper. Chill. Store in refrigerator.

To dip candies, centres should be at room temperature or chocolate will cool down too quickly. Using a fork with long tines, place centres, one at a time in chocolate to cover completely. Lift with fork and remove excess chocolate on side of bowl. Place on waxed paper-lined baking sheet. Chill. Store in refrigerator.

MOST ASKED QUESTIONS . . . .
OF THE BAKER'S KITCHENS

1. *When a recipe specifies either one ounce of chocolate, or one square of chocolate, does it refer to one wrapped square or ½ square?*

    One ounce of chocolate or one square of chocolate is one whole individually wrapped square.

    ◆

2. *Can BAKER'S Semi-Sweet Chocolate be substituted for BAKER'S Unsweetened Chocolate or vice versa?*

    No. Never substitute one chocolate for another in a recipe as this will affect the flavour and may cause the dessert to fail.

    ◆

3. *Can BAKER'S Semi-Sweet Chocolate Chips be substituted for semi-sweet squares?*

    No. Chocolate chips are formulated to keep their shape when baked. Chocolate chips when melted are very thick and therefore not a suitable texture for substitution.

    ◆

4. *What is BAKER'S GERMAN'S Sweet Chocolate and where can it be obtained?*

    BAKER'S GERMAN'S Sweet Chocolate is available only in the United States, but BAKER'S Sweet Chocolate, available in Canada, can be substituted for it in any recipe, as they are the same product.

    Canadian BAKER'S Sweet Chocolate is sold in a 225 g or an 8 oz package while the American BAKER'S GERMAN'S Sweet Chocolate is sold in a 4 oz package. This fact is important when substituting, as some recipes call for half a package.

    ◆

5. *Some recipes call for toasted nuts. How do I toast nuts?*

    To toast, spread nuts in a single layer on a cookie sheet. Bake at 350°F (180°C) for 10 minutes (pecans and walnuts) to 20 minutes (whole almonds). Cool in pan on wire rack. Store in refrigerator until ready to use.

    ◆

6. *Can chocolate purchased in bulk food stores be substituted for BAKER'S Chocolate?*

    Most of the chocolate sold at bulk food stores is not pure chocolate but compound chocolate which is manufactured with a mixture of fats including vegetable oils. It is often cheaper to purchase and has noticeably less chocolate flavour delivery. Its performance in recipes would not equal that of BAKER'S pure chocolate.

KID'S TREATS

CHOCOLATE SPIDERS

A favourite after school treat – a spider made from chocolate!

6	squares BAKER'S Semi-Sweet Chocolate, chopped	6	
1 cup	BAKER'S Butterscotch Chips	250 mL	
2 cups	chow mein noodles	500 mL	
1 cup	salted peanuts	250 mL	
1 cup	KRAFT Miniature Marshmallows	250 mL	

◆ Melt chocolate and butterscotch chips over hot water, or in microwave on MEDIUM power 3 to 4 minutes, stirring until smooth.

◆ Add noodles, peanuts and marshmallows, stirring until coated with chocolate mixture.

◆ Drop from teaspoon onto wax paper-lined pan. Chill until firm. Store in airtight container in refrigerator.

Prep time: 15 minutes plus chilling
Makes about 3 dozen spiders.

Note: To give spiders 'eyes', decorate each spider with two small round candies before chilling.

CHOCOLATE MUNCH MIX

Pack this in the kids' lunchboxes for an anytime snack!

1 pkg (300 g)	BAKER'S Semi-Sweet Chocolate Chips	1 pkg (300 g)	
2 cups	nuts (peanuts, cashews, almonds)	500 mL	
2 cups	raisins	500 mL	

◆ Combine all ingredients; mix well. Store in airtight container.

Prep time: 5 minutes
Makes 6 cups (1.5 L).

FROZEN FLYING SAUCERS

Better than an ice cream sandwich and a lot more fun!

4	squares BAKER'S Semi-Sweet Chocolate, chopped	4
¼ cup	water	50 mL
1	envelope DREAM WHIP Dessert Topping, prepared	1
32	baked BAKER'S Best Chocolate Chip Cookies made with oats (see page 47)	32

◆ Melt chocolate with water in microwave on MEDIUM power 2 to 4 minutes, or on stove over low heat. Stir until completely melted and smooth. Cool.

◆ Fold dessert topping into chocolate mixture.

◆ Place a dollop of chocolate topping onto bottoms of 16 cookies. Place remaining cookies on top, forming a sandwich.

◆ Freeze filled cookies until firm, about 3 hours.

Prep time: 15 minutes plus chilling
Makes 16 saucers.

Note: These keep well in freezer up to 3 months.

CHOCOLATE POPCORN METEORS

Crunchy chocolate-coated popcorn – great for video night!

12 cups	popped popcorn	3 L
1 cup	unsalted peanuts	250 mL
1 cup	sugar	250 mL
⅔ cup	corn syrup	150 mL
2 Tbsp	butter or margarine	30 mL
6	squares BAKER'S Semi-Sweet Chocolate	6

◆ Heat oven to 250°F (120°C).

◆ Mix popcorn and peanuts in large shallow roasting pan.

◆ Cook sugar, corn syrup and butter in heavy 2 qt (2 L) saucepan over medium heat until mixture boils, stirring constantly.

◆ Stir in chocolate. Cook, stirring constantly, 5 minutes or until chocolate is completely melted and mixture is very thick. Remove from heat. Pour over popcorn; stir to coat well.

◆ Bake for 1 hour, stirring occasionally. Pour popcorn in single layer onto cookie sheets or foil; cool. Store in tightly covered containers.

Prep time: 15 minutes
Baking time: 1 hour
Makes about 12 cups (3 L).

CHOCOLATE BANANA POPS

These won't last long in the freezer!

6	medium-size ripe bananas	6
6	squares BAKER'S Semi-Sweet Chocolate, chopped	6
⅓ cup	butter or margarine	75 mL
¼ cup	hot water	50 mL
	Finely chopped nuts or toasted coconut (optional)	

◆ Cut bananas in half crosswise. Insert a wooden stick in cut end of each banana half and freeze until firm, about 3 hours.

◆ Melt chocolate and butter in a bowl set over hot water. Blend in ¼ cup (50 mL) hot water. Pour chocolate mixture into a tall narrow glass.

◆ Dip in frozen bananas to coat evenly. Immediately roll in finely chopped nuts or toasted coconut, if desired. Place on wax paper-lined pan. Serve immediately or store covered in freezer.

Prep time: 15 minutes plus freezing
Makes 12 pops.

Peanutty Oatmeal Chunk Cookies

Serve these with a glass of milk for a yummy after school snack.

1½ cups	KRAFT Crunchy or Smooth Peanut Butter	375 mL
½ cup	butter or margarine, softened	125 mL
¾ cup	sugar	175 mL
⅔ cup	packed brown sugar	150 mL
2	eggs	2
1½ tsp	vanilla	7 mL
1 cup	quick-cooking rolled oats	250 mL
¾ cup	all-purpose flour	175 mL
½ tsp	baking soda	2 mL
8	squares BAKER'S Semi-Sweet Chocolate, each square cut into 8 pieces	8

◆ Heat oven to 350°F (180°C).

◆ In mixing bowl, cream together peanut butter and butter. Gradually beat in sugars. Blend in eggs and vanilla.

◆ Mix oats, flour and baking soda. Blend into creamed mixture, just until combined. Stir in chocolate chunks. Drop by tablespoonfuls onto ungreased cookie sheets.

◆ Bake for 10 to 12 minutes or until centres are still soft to touch. Cool 3 minutes; transfer to rack to cool.

Prep time: 15 minutes
Baking time: 12 minutes
Makes about 3½ dozen cookies.

Chewy Peanut Butter Mini-Chippers

¾ cup	packed brown sugar	175 mL
½ cup	butter or margarine, softened	125 mL
⅓ cup	KRAFT Crunchy or Smooth Peanut Butter	75 mL
¼ cup	sugar	50 mL
1 tsp	vanilla	5 mL
1	egg	1
¾ cup	all-purpose flour	175 mL
½ tsp	baking soda	2 mL
¼ tsp	salt	1 mL
1 cup	BAKER'S Miniature Semi-Sweet Chocolate Chips	250 mL

◆ Heat oven to 375°F (190°C).

◆ Combine brown sugar, butter, peanut butter, sugar, vanilla and egg. Beat on low speed of electric mixer until well blended.

◆ Stir in flour, baking soda and salt. Stir in chips.

◆ Drop by heaping tablespoonfuls onto ungreased cookie sheets.

◆ Bake for 8 to 10 minutes or until cookies are golden brown around the edges and appear slightly underbaked in the centre. Transfer to rack to cool.

Prep time: 15 minutes
Baking time: 10 minutes
Makes about 20 large cookies.

Chewy Peanut Butter Mini-Chippers   *Peanutty Oatmeal Chunk Cookies*

OATMEAL FUNNY FACE COOKIES

*This recipe will entertain children for hours and
Mom and Dad will be impressed with the creative results.*

Cookie

2⅓ cups	quick-cooking rolled oats	575 mL
1½ cups	all-purpose flour	375 mL
2 tsp	baking soda	10 mL
1 tsp	salt	5 mL
1 cup	butter or margarine	250 mL
1½ cups	packed brown sugar	375 mL
2	eggs	2
1 tsp	vanilla	5 mL
1½ cups	BAKER'S Miniature Semi-Sweet Chocolate Chips	375 mL
1 cup	chopped nuts	250 mL

Decoration

3	squares BAKER'S Unsweetened Chocolate, melted	3
2 Tbsp	butter or margarine	30 mL
2¼ cups	sifted icing sugar	550 mL
⅓ cup	milk	75 mL
	Candies: gum drops, licorice, jelly beans, etc.	

Cookie:

◆ Heat oven to 350°F (180°C).

◆ Combine oats, flour, baking soda and salt. Stir well to blend.

◆ Cream butter, brown sugar, eggs and vanilla. Add dry ingredients; mix well. Stir in chocolate chips and nuts.

◆ Drop dough by heaping tablespoonfuls on lightly greased cookie sheets. Flatten with fingers to 3½ inch (9 cm) circles.

◆ Bake for 10 to 15 minutes or until golden.

◆ Cool on pans 5 minutes, then transfer to racks to cool completely.

Decoration:

◆ Beat first 4 ingredients together to make a smooth, spreadable chocolate icing.

◆ Spread on cookies and use your favourite candies or any other decorations to make faces.

Prep time: 30 minutes
Baking time: 15 minutes
Makes about 25 cookies.

Combine oats, flour, baking soda and salt. Stir.

Cream butter, sugar, eggs and vanilla.

Add dry ingredients and mix well.

Stir in chips and nuts.

Drop spoonfuls of dough onto cookie sheet and flatten with fingers.

Decorate cookies with icing and assorted candies.

ROCKY ROAD BARS

One of our most favourite treats.

1½ cups	graham crumbs	375 mL
½ cup	butter or margarine, melted	125 mL
1½ cups	BAKER'S ANGEL FLAKE Coconut	375 mL
1½ cups	chopped nuts	375 mL
1 pkg (300 g)	BAKER'S Semi-Sweet Chocolate Chips	1 pkg (300 g)
1½ cups	KRAFT Miniature Marshmallows	375 mL
1 can (300 mL)	sweetened condensed milk	1 can (300 mL)
3	squares BAKER'S Semi-Sweet Chocolate, melted	3

◆ Heat oven to 350°F (180°C).

◆ Combine crumbs and butter. Press into 13 × 9 inch (33 × 23 cm) pan. Layer coconut, nuts, chocolate chips and marshmallows evenly over crumbs. Drizzle condensed milk evenly over the top.

◆ Bake for 25 to 30 minutes or until golden brown. Remove from oven, drizzle with melted chocolate; cool.

Prep time: 15 minutes
Baking time: 30 minutes
Makes 36 bars.

BROWNIES BONANZA

ONE-BOWL BROWNIES

BAKER'S easiest ever brownies.

Brownies

4	squares BAKER'S Unsweetened Chocolate	4
¾ cup	butter or margarine	175 mL
2 cups	sugar	500 mL
3	eggs	3
1 tsp	vanilla	5 mL
1 cup	all-purpose flour	250 mL
1 cup	chopped nuts (optional)	250 mL

Icing

2	squares BAKER'S Unsweetened Chocolate	2
2 Tbsp	butter	30 mL
¼ cup	milk	50 mL
2 cups	icing sugar, sifted	500 mL

Brownies:

◆ Heat oven to 350°F (180°C).

◆ Heat chocolate and butter over low heat or in microwave on HIGH 2 minutes until butter is melted. Stir until completely smooth. Stir sugar into chocolate. Mix in eggs and vanilla until well blended. Stir in flour and nuts. Spread in greased 13 × 9 inch (33 × 23 cm) metal* pan.

◆ Bake 35 to 40 minutes or until cake tester inserted in centre comes out almost clean. Do not overbake. Cool in pan.

Icing:

◆ Melt chocolate with butter and milk; blend until smooth. Add icing sugar; blend well. Spread over brownies; cut into squares.

Prep time: 7 minutes
Baking time: 40 minutes
Makes 24 brownies.

* If using a glass pan reduce heat to 325°F (160°C).

VARIATIONS:

For cake-like brownies: Stir in ½ cup (125 mL) milk with eggs and vanilla. Increase flour to 1½ cups (375 mL).

For fudgy brownies: Use 4 eggs. Bake 30 to 35 minutes.

For extra thick brownies: Bake in 9 inch (23 cm) square metal pan at 325°F (160°C) for 50 minutes.

German Chocolate Cream Cheese Brownies

4	squares BAKER'S Sweet Chocolate	4
¼ cup	butter or margarine	50 mL
¾ cup	sugar	175 mL
2	eggs, beaten	2
1 tsp	vanilla	5 mL
½ cup	all-purpose flour	125 mL
½ cup	chopped nuts	125 mL
1 pkg (125 g)	PHILADELPHIA BRAND Cream Cheese, softened	1 pkg (125 g)
¼ cup	sugar	50 mL
1	egg	1
1 Tbsp	all-purpose flour	15 mL

◆ Heat oven to 350°F (180°C).

◆ Microwave chocolate and butter in large bowl on HIGH 2 minutes or until butter is melted. Stir until chocolate is completely melted.

◆ Add ¾ cup (175 mL) sugar; mix well. Blend in two eggs and vanilla. Stir in ½ cup (125 mL) flour and nuts; mix well. Spread into greased 8 inch (20 cm) square baking pan.

◆ In small bowl, beat cream cheese, ¼ cup (50 mL) sugar, 1 egg and 1 Tbsp (15 mL) flour until well blended. Spoon over brownie mixture; cut through batter with knife several times for marble effect.

◆ Bake 35 to 40 minutes or until cake tester inserted in centre comes out almost clean. Do not overbake. Cool. Cut into squares.

Prep time: 15 minutes
Baking time: 40 minutes
Makes 16 brownies.

BAKER'S CLASSIC BROWNIES

An old-fashioned moist and chewy brownie.

2	squares BAKER'S Unsweetened Chocolate	2
⅓ cup	butter or margarine	75 mL
⅔ cup	all-purpose flour	150 mL
½ tsp	baking powder	2 mL
¼ tsp	salt	1 mL
2	eggs	2
1 cup	sugar	250 mL
1 tsp	vanilla	5 mL
½ cup	chopped nuts	125 mL

◆ Heat oven to 350°F (180°C).

◆ Melt chocolate with butter over hot water; cool.

◆ Sift flour with baking powder and salt.

◆ Beat eggs. Gradually add sugar, beating until well blended. Blend in chocolate mixture and vanilla. Stir in flour mixture. Fold in nuts. Spread into greased and floured 8 inch (20 cm) square pan.

◆ Bake for 25 to 30 minutes or until brownies begin to pull away from sides of pan. Cool in pan on rack.

Prep time: 20 minutes
Baking time: 30 minutes
Makes about 16 brownies.

VARIATIONS:

Delicately Dusted: Sprinkle icing sugar evenly over cooled brownies.

Nuttier Than Ever: Sprinkle with ½ cup (125 mL) chopped nuts before baking.

Gloriously Glazed: Melt 1 square BAKER'S Unsweetened Chocolate with 1 Tbsp (15 mL) butter and ¼ cup (50 mL) milk; blend until smooth. Add 1¼ cups (300 mL) sifted icing sugar; blend well. Spread over cooled brownies.

Really Rocky Road: Sprinkle still warm brownies with 2 cups (500 mL) KRAFT Miniature Marshmallows. Broil under pre-heated broiler until marshmallows are golden brown. Melt 1 square BAKER'S Semi-Sweet Chocolate with 1 tsp (5 mL) butter over low heat. Using a small spoon, drizzle in a random pattern over marshmallows.

PEANUT BUTTER SWIRLED BROWNIES

Peanut butter and chocolate – these are fabulous!

Brownies

2	squares BAKER'S Unsweetened Chocolate	2
⅓ cup	butter or margarine	75 mL
⅔ cup	all-purpose flour	150 mL
½ tsp	baking powder	2 mL
¼ tsp	salt	1 mL
2	eggs	2
1 cup	sugar	250 mL
1 tsp	vanilla	5 mL
½ cup	KRAFT Smooth Peanut Butter	125 mL
¼ cup	sugar	50 mL
¼ cup	milk	50 mL

Icing

4	squares BAKER'S Semi-Sweet Chocolate, chopped	4
¾ cup	KRAFT Smooth Peanut Butter, divided	175 mL

Brownies:

◆ Heat oven to 350°F (180°C).

◆ Heat chocolate with butter over low heat or in microwave on HIGH 1 minute until butter is melted. Stir until chocolate is completely melted; cool.

◆ Combine flour with baking powder and salt. Set aside.

◆ Beat eggs. Gradually add 1 cup (250 mL) sugar, beating until well blended. Blend in cooled chocolate mixture and vanilla. Stir in flour mixture. Spread into greased and floured 8 inch (20 cm) square pan.

◆ Combine peanut butter, ¼ cup (50 mL) sugar and milk; blend well. Top brownies with spoonfuls of peanut butter mixture. Draw knife through batter to marble.

◆ Bake 35 to 40 minutes or until brownies begin to pull away from sides of pan. Cool in pan on rack.

Icing:

◆ Melt chocolate with ½ cup (125 mL) KRAFT Peanut Butter over low heat or in microwave on MEDIUM power for 3 minutes. Stir until well blended. Spread over top of cooled brownies.

◆ Melt remaining peanut butter as above and drop by spoonfuls onto icing. Swirl with knife to marble. Chill until set.

Prep time: 25 minutes
Baking time: 40 minutes
Makes 16 brownies.

FUDGY CREAM CHEESE BROWNIES

Chocolate Batter

½ cup	all-purpose flour	125 mL
½ tsp	baking powder	2 mL
¼ tsp	salt	1 mL
4	squares BAKER'S Semi-Sweet Chocolate	4
3 Tbsp	butter or margarine	45 mL
2	eggs	2
¾ cup	sugar	175 mL
1 tsp	vanilla	5 mL

Cream Cheese Batter

1 pkg (125 g)	PHILADELPHIA BRAND Cream Cheese, softened	1 pkg (125 g)
2 Tbsp	butter, softened	30 mL
1 tsp	vanilla	5 mL
¼ cup	sugar	50 mL
1	egg	1

Chocolate Batter:

- ◆ Heat oven to 350°F (180°C).
- ◆ Combine flour, baking powder, and salt.
- ◆ Melt chocolate with butter over low heat or in microwave on MEDIUM power 3 minutes.
- ◆ Beat eggs until foamy. Gradually add sugar; continue beating at medium speed of electric mixer until thick and lemon-coloured, about 5 minutes. Add vanilla and chocolate mixture; mix well. Add flour mixture; mix well.

Cream Cheese Batter:

- ◆ Beat cream cheese with remaining ingredients until well blended.
- ◆ Layer half of chocolate batter in greased and floured 8 inch (20 cm) square pan.
- ◆ Spread with cheese mixture. Top with spoonfuls of chocolate batter. Draw knife through layers to marble.
- ◆ Bake for 35 minutes or until brownies pull away from sides of pan. Cool on rack.

Prep time: 30 minutes
Baking time: 35 minutes
Makes about 16 brownies.

NO-BAKE BROWNIES

Too hot to bake? Try these no-bake goodies and keep your cool.

1 cup	chopped pecans or walnuts	250 mL
4 cups	graham crumbs	1 L
½ cup	icing sugar	125 mL
8	squares BAKER'S Semi-Sweet Chocolate, chopped	8
1 cup	evaporated milk	250 mL
1 tsp	vanilla	5 mL

- ◆ Combine nuts, crumbs and icing sugar in large mixing bowl; mix well.
- ◆ Melt chocolate with milk over hot water; add vanilla and mix well.
- ◆ Set aside ½ cup (125 mL) chocolate mixture. Stir crumb mixture into remaining chocolate mixture; mix well.
- ◆ Spread in greased 9 inch (23 cm) square pan. Spread remaining chocolate evenly over surface. Chill.

Prep time: 15 minutes plus chilling
Makes 30 brownies.

BLONDIES

White chocolate brownies.

¼ cup	butter	50 mL
4	squares BAKER'S White Chocolate, coarsely chopped	4
2	eggs	2
½ cup	sugar	125 mL
1 tsp	vanilla	5 mL
¾ cup	all-purpose flour	175 mL
	Pinch salt	
½ cup	slivered almonds	125 mL
2	squares BAKER'S White Chocolate, coarsely chopped	2

◆ Heat oven to 325°F (160°C).

◆ Line an 8 inch (20 cm) square pan with foil and grease.

◆ Melt butter over low heat. Remove from heat and stir in 4 squares chocolate. Stir until smooth.

◆ Beat eggs, sugar and vanilla until thick and lemon-coloured. Add chocolate mixture. Blend in flour, salt, almonds and remaining chocolate. Pour into prepared pan.

◆ Bake for 30 to 35 minutes, until lightly golden. Cool. Remove brownies from pan. Peel away foil; cut into squares.

Prep time: 20 minutes
Baking time: 35 minutes
Makes about 16 squares.

Mississippi Mud Brownies

Ooey and gooey – the name says it all!

Brownies

4	squares BAKER'S Unsweetened Chocolate	4
¾ cup	butter or margarine	175 mL
2 cups	sugar	500 mL
3	eggs	3
1 tsp	vanilla	5 mL
1 cup	all-purpose flour	250 mL
1 cup	pecans, coarsely chopped	250 mL
1 cup	BAKER'S Semi-Sweet Chocolate Chips	250 mL
3 cups	KRAFT Miniature Marshmallows	750 mL

Icing

2	squares BAKER'S Unsweetened Chocolate, chopped	2
2 Tbsp	butter	30 mL
¼ cup	milk	50 mL
2 cups	icing sugar, sifted	500 mL

Brownies:

◆ Heat oven to 350°F (180°C).

◆ Heat chocolate with butter over low heat or in microwave on HIGH 2 minutes until butter is melted. Stir until chocolate is completely melted. Stir sugar into melted chocolate until well blended. Add eggs and vanilla; stir until completely mixed. Stir in flour until well blended. Stir in nuts and chocolate chips. Spread in greased 13 × 9 inch (33 × 23 cm) pan.

◆ Bake for 25 to 30 minutes or until brownies begin to pull away from sides of pan.

◆ Remove from oven and immediately sprinkle marshmallows over the top. Return to oven and bake 5 minutes more. Remove from oven and cool on rack.

Icing:

◆ Melt chocolate with butter and milk over low heat or in microwave on HIGH 2 minutes; blend until smooth. Add icing sugar; blend well.

◆ Spread icing over marshmallow layer.

Prep time: 20 minutes
Baking time: 35 minutes
Makes 24 brownies.

Stir sugar into melted chocolate.

Stir in eggs and vanilla.

Stir in flour.

Mix in nuts and chips.

Sprinkle marshmallows over
top of baked brownies.

Spread icing over marshmallow
layer.

BROWNIE CHEESECAKE CUPCAKES

*With these individual decadent treats
you'll be a hit at your next get-together!*

Cheese Mixture

1 pkg (250 g)	PHILADELPHIA BRAND Cream Cheese, softened	1 pkg (250 g)
⅓ cup	sugar	75 mL
1 Tbsp	all-purpose flour	15 mL
1	egg	1
1 cup	BAKER'S Miniature Semi-Sweet Chocolate Chips	250 mL

Brownies

8	squares BAKER'S Unsweetened Chocolate	8
1½ cups	butter or margarine	375 mL
6	eggs	6
3 cups	sugar	750 mL
1½ cups	all-purpose flour	375 mL
1 cup	BAKER'S Miniature Semi-Sweet Chocolate Chips	250 mL

Cheese Mixture:

◆ Beat cream cheese, sugar and flour until smooth. Beat in egg, just until combined. Fold in chips. Chill while preparing cupcakes.

Brownies:

◆ Heat oven to 350°F (180°C).

◆ Melt chocolate and butter over low heat or in microwave on MEDIUM power for 4 minutes. Cool.

◆ Beat eggs in large bowl on high speed with electric mixer until lemon-coloured. Gradually add sugar, beating until thick, about 3 minutes. Stir in melted chocolate mixture. Fold in flour.

◆ Pour into 24 paper-lined muffin cups (or 48 small muffin tins). Place a heaping teaspoon of cheese mixture into the centre of each brownie. Sprinkle brownies with remaining chocolate chips.

◆ Bake for 25 to 30 minutes. Do not overbake. These cupcakes should be very moist in the centre.

*Prep time: 25 minutes
Baking time: 30 minutes
Makes 24 regular or 48 small individual brownies.*

RICH ESPRESSO BROWNIE BARS

Brownie

3	squares BAKER'S Unsweetened Chocolate	3
2	squares BAKER'S Semi-Sweet Chocolate	2
½ cup	butter or margarine	125 mL
2	eggs	2
1	egg, separated	1
1¼ cups	packed brown sugar	300 mL
¾ cup	all-purpose flour	175 mL
¼ tsp	baking powder	1 mL
⅓ cup	coarsely chopped toasted pecans	75 mL

Cream Cheese Topping

3 pkgs (125 g each)	PHILADELPHIA BRAND Cream Cheese, softened	3 pkgs (125 g each)
1 cup	icing sugar, sifted	250 mL
2 Tbsp	instant coffee granules	30 mL
1 Tbsp	coffee liqueur	15 mL
1	egg	1
1	square BAKER'S Semi-Sweet Chocolate	1
1 tsp	vegetable oil	5 mL

Brownie:

◆ Melt chocolate and butter over low heat or in microwave on MEDIUM power 3 minutes until butter is melted; cool.

◆ Beat 2 whole eggs, 1 egg yolk and sugar on highest speed of electric mixer for 5 minutes.

◆ Fold in chocolate mixture and remaining brownie ingredients.

◆ Pour into greased and floured 13 × 9 inch (33 × 23 cm) pan; chill for 15 minutes.

Cream Cheese Topping:

◆ Heat oven to 325°F (160°C).

◆ Combine cream cheese, icing sugar, coffee, liqueur, whole egg and the remaining egg white.

◆ Beat at lowest speed of electric mixer until well blended. Spread over batter in pan.

◆ Melt chocolate square and oil; cool to room temperature. Drizzle chocolate in lines, ¾ inch (2 cm) apart horizontally down length of pan. Using a toothpick, start from bottom corner of pan and draw it back and forth at ½ inch (1 cm) intervals vertically to create "feather" effect.

◆ Bake for 30 minutes or until cream cheese mixture is set. Cool. Cut into bars or squares. Store any leftover bars in refrigerator.

Prep time: 30 minutes
Baking time: 30 minutes.

Pour brownie batter into prepared pan.

2

Spread cream cheese topping over brownie layer.

3

Drizzle melted chocolate in lines down length of pan.

4

Draw toothpick through lines back and forth to "feather".

BLOCKBUSTER BROWNIES

Our decadent gourmet brownies for the true connoisseur.

8	squares BAKER'S Unsweetened Chocolate	8
1½ cups	butter or margarine	375 mL
6	eggs	6
3 cups	sugar	750 mL
1½ cups	all-purpose flour	375 mL
1 Tbsp	vanilla	15 mL
1 cup	chopped pecans or walnuts	250 mL

◆ Heat oven to 350°F (180°C).

◆ Melt chocolate and butter over low heat or in microwave on MEDIUM power 4 minutes; cool.

◆ Beat eggs until lemon-coloured. Gradually add sugar, beating until thick, about 3 minutes. Stir in chocolate mixture. Fold in flour, vanilla and nuts. Pour into *two* greased and floured 8 inch (20 cm) square pans.

◆ Bake for 35 to 40 minutes. Do not overbake. These brownies should be very moist in the centre. Halve recipe for 1 pan. Freezes well.

Prep time: 15 minutes
Baking time: 35 to 40 minutes
Makes about 32 brownies.

VARIATIONS:

See topping variations provided in Baker's Classic Brownie page 29.

COOKIES AND SQUARES

CHOCOLATE-TOPPED CRUNCHIES

These will remind you of your favourite chocolate bar.

⅓ cup	packed brown sugar	75 mL
3 Tbsp	corn syrup	45 mL
2 Tbsp	KRAFT Crunchy Peanut Butter	30 mL
2 Tbsp	melted butter or margarine	30 mL
½ tsp	vanilla	2 mL
2 cups	bran flake cereal	500 mL
4	squares BAKER'S Semi-Sweet Chocolate, chopped	4
⅓ cup	KRAFT Crunchy Peanut Butter	75 mL

◆ Heat oven to 375°F (190°C).

◆ Combine brown sugar, corn syrup, 2 Tbsp (30 mL) peanut butter, butter and vanilla; mix well. Add cereal, mixing well. Press into greased 8 inch (20 cm) square pan. Bake for 5 minutes.

◆ Melt chocolate and remaining peanut butter over low heat. Spread evenly over baked layer. Chill and cut into bars. Store in refrigerator.

Prep time: 10 minutes
Baking time: 5 minutes
Makes about 32 bars.

JUMBO OATMEAL CHOCOLATE CHIP COOKIES

1 cup	butter or margarine	250 mL
1½ cups	packed brown sugar	375 mL
2	eggs	2
1 tsp	vanilla	5 mL
1½ cups	all-purpose flour	375 mL
2⅓ cups	quick-cooking rolled oats	575 mL
2 tsp	baking soda	10 mL
1 tsp	salt	5 mL
1 pkg (300 g)	BAKER'S Semi-Sweet Chocolate Chips	1 pkg (300 g)
1 cup	raisins	250 mL

◆ Heat oven to 350°F (180°C).

◆ Cream together butter and sugar until light and fluffy. Beat in eggs and vanilla. Add flour, oats, baking soda and salt; mix until well blended. Stir in chips and raisins.

◆ Drop dough in ¼ cup (50 mL) mounds onto greased cookie sheets, about 3 inches (7.5 cm) apart. Flatten each cookie into a 2½ inch (6 cm) circle.

◆ Bake for 15 to 20 minutes or until edges brown lightly. Cool 5 minutes; transfer to racks to cool thoroughly.

Prep time: 20 minutes
Baking time: 20 minutes
Makes about 20 large cookies.

Note: This dough stores well in the freezer. Try using a small ¼ cup (50 mL) ice cream scoop to drop the dough onto the cookie sheets.

PEANUT BUTTER WHITE CHOCOLATE PECAN COOKIES

1 cup	all-purpose flour	250 mL
½ tsp	baking soda	2 mL
¼ tsp	salt	1 mL
½ cup	KRAFT Chunky Peanut Butter	125 mL
½ cup	butter or margarine	125 mL
½ cup	packed brown sugar	125 mL
2 Tbsp	sugar	30 mL
1	egg	1
1 tsp	vanilla	5 mL
6	squares BAKER'S White Chocolate, coarsely chopped	6
1 cup	pecans, coarsely chopped and toasted	250 mL

◆ Heat oven to 375°F (190°C).

◆ Stir flour, baking soda and salt together. Set aside.

◆ Beat peanut butter, butter and sugars in a large mixing bowl for 4 minutes or until very creamy. Add the egg and vanilla, beat until fluffy, about 3 minutes.

◆ Using a wooden spoon, stir in the flour mixture until thoroughly mixed. Stir in chocolate and nuts.

◆ Drop by heaping tablespoonfuls onto 2 large ungreased cookie sheets about 1 inch (2.5 cm) apart. Flatten dough mounds with your fingers.

◆ Bake for 9 to 10 minutes. Do not overbake. Cool 5 minutes; transfer to rack to cool. Store cookies in airtight container.

Prep time: 15 minutes
Baking time: 10 minutes
Makes 2½ dozen cookies.

CLASSIC CHOCOLATE CHIP COOKIES

*We still get requests for this one – our old package recipe
from years ago!*

⅓ cup	butter or margarine, softened	75 mL
⅓ cup	shortening	75 mL
½ cup	sugar	125 mL
½ cup	packed brown sugar	125 mL
1	egg	1
1 tsp	vanilla	5 mL
1¼ cups	all-purpose flour	300 mL
½ tsp	baking soda	2 mL
¼ tsp	salt	1 mL
1 pkg (175 g)	BAKER'S Semi-Sweet Chocolate Chips	1 pkg (175 g)

◆ Heat oven to 375°F (190°C).

◆ Beat butter, shortening, sugar, brown sugar, egg, and vanilla until light and fluffy. Add flour, baking soda, and salt; blend well. Stir in chocolate chips.

◆ Drop by heaping teaspoonfuls onto ungreased cookie sheets.

◆ Bake for 10 to 12 minutes. Transfer to rack to cool.

Prep time: 10 minutes
Baking time: 12 minutes
Makes about 40 cookies.

OATMEAL BUTTERSCOTCH CHIP COOKIES

½ cup	butter or margarine, softened	125 mL
½ cup	sugar	125 mL
¼ cup	packed brown sugar	50 mL
1 tsp	vanilla	5 mL
1	egg	1
1 cup	quick-cooking rolled oats	250 mL
1 cup	all-purpose flour	250 mL
½ tsp	*each* baking soda and salt	2 mL
1 pkg (300 g)	BAKER'S Butterscotch Chips	1 pkg (300 g)

◆ Heat oven to 350°F (180°C).

◆ Beat butter, sugars, vanilla and egg until light and fluffy.

◆ Mix in rolled oats, flour, baking soda and salt by hand until well blended. Stir in butterscotch chips.

◆ Drop by heaping teaspoonfuls onto ungreased cookie sheets, placing 2 inches (5 cm) apart.

◆ Bake for 10 to 12 minutes or until lightly browned. Cookies will be soft in centre when done. Cool 2 minutes before removing to rack. Cool.

Prep time: 10 minutes
Baking time: 12 minutes
Makes 36 cookies.

1 Beat butter, sugars, vanilla and eggs with electric mixer.

2 Stir in dry ingredients by hand.

3 Stir in chips and nuts.

BAKER'S BEST CHOCOLATE CHIP COOKIES

Our famous package recipe.

1 cup	butter or margarine, softened	250 mL
1 cup	packed brown sugar	250 mL
½ cup	sugar	125 mL
2 tsp	vanilla	10 mL
2	eggs	2
2¼ cups	all-purpose flour	550 mL
1 tsp	baking soda	5 mL
½ tsp	salt	2 mL
1 pkg (300 g)	BAKER'S Semi-Sweet Chocolate Chips	1 pkg (300 g)
1 cup	chopped pecans or walnuts (optional)	250 mL

◆ Heat oven to 375°F (190°C).

◆ Beat butter, sugars, vanilla and eggs until light and fluffy.

◆ Mix in flour, baking soda and salt by hand until well blended.

◆ Stir in chocolate chips and nuts. Drop by heaping teaspoonfuls onto ungreased cookie sheet 2 inches (5 cm) apart.

◆ Bake for 10 to 12 minutes, or until lightly browned. Transfer to rack to cool.

Prep time: 10 minutes
Baking time: 12 minutes
Makes about 5 dozen cookies.

VARIATION:

Add 1 cup (250 mL) quick-cooking rolled oats or BAKER'S ANGEL FLAKE Coconut to batter.

Drop by teaspoonfuls onto cookie sheets.

CHOCOLATE-DIPPED MACAROONS

4	large egg whites, at room temperature	4
1½ tsp	vanilla	7 mL
⅔ cup	sugar	150 mL
¼ cup	all-purpose flour	50 mL
3½ cups	lightly packed BAKER'S ANGEL FLAKE Coconut	875 mL
6	squares BAKER'S Semi-Sweet Chocolate, chopped	6
3 Tbsp	butter or margarine	45 mL

◆ Heat oven to 325°F (160°C).

◆ In a large bowl, beat egg whites with an electric mixer until frothy. Add vanilla, sugar, and flour; mix until smooth.

◆ Stir in coconut until evenly moistened.

◆ On 2 well-greased baking sheets, evenly space ¼ cup (50 mL) portions of dough. Pat each into a flat-topped circle about 3 inches (7.5 cm) in diameter. Bake until macaroons are golden and only slightly wet-looking, about 25 minutes. Transfer macaroons to racks and let cool.

◆ Melt chocolate and butter over low heat or in microwave on MEDIUM power for 2 minutes. Stir until completely melted.

◆ Dip half of each macaroon in chocolate. Set macaroons on wax paper-lined cookie sheet. Chill, uncovered, until chocolate hardens, about 45 minutes. Store in airtight container for up to 1 week.

Prep time: 20 minutes plus chilling
Baking time: 25 minutes
Makes 10 macaroons.

Peanut Butter Nanaimo Bars

Base		
½ cup	butter or margarine	125 mL
3	squares BAKER'S Semi-Sweet Chocolate, chopped	3
2 Tbsp	sugar	30 mL
1 tsp	vanilla	5 mL
1	egg	1
2 cups	graham crumbs	500 mL
1 cup	BAKER'S ANGEL FLAKE Coconut	250 mL
½ cup	chopped nuts	125 mL

Filling		
2 Tbsp	custard powder	30 mL
¼ cup	milk	50 mL
2 Tbsp	butter, softened	30 mL
½ cup	KRAFT Smooth Peanut Butter	125 mL
2 cups	icing sugar, sifted	500 mL

Icing		
5	squares BAKER'S Semi-Sweet Chocolate, chopped	5
1 Tbsp	butter	15 mL

Base:

◆ Melt butter and chocolate in microwave on HIGH for 2 minutes, or over low heat. Mix in sugar, vanilla and egg. Add crumbs, coconut and nuts; mix well. Press into 9 inch (23 cm) square pan. Chill.

Filling:

◆ Using electric mixer beat together all ingredients. Spread over base; chill.

Icing:

◆ Melt chocolate with butter over low heat or in microwave on MEDIUM power 3 to 4 minutes. Spread over filling.

Prep time: 20 minutes plus chilling
Makes about 18 bars.

WHITE CHOCOLATE CHIP COOKIES

The reverse chocolate chip cookie!

5	squares BAKER'S Semi-Sweet Chocolate	5
½ cup	butter or margarine	125 mL
1	egg	1
½ cup	sugar	125 mL
½ cup	packed brown sugar	125 mL
1 tsp	vanilla	5 mL
1⅔ cups	all-purpose flour	400 mL
½ tsp	baking soda	2 mL
½ tsp	baking powder	2 mL
½ tsp	salt	2 mL
¼ cup	sour cream	50 mL
1 pkg (225 g)	BAKER'S White Chocolate Chips	1 pkg (225 g)

◆ Melt semi-sweet chocolate with butter over low heat or in microwave on HIGH 2 minutes.

◆ Beat egg with sugars and vanilla until well blended. Beat in chocolate mixture. Mix in flour, baking soda, baking powder, salt and sour cream until well blended. Stir in chocolate chips.

◆ Chill dough for at least 30 minutes to harden and prevent spreading of cookies.

◆ Heat oven to 350°F (180°C).

◆ Drop by heaping teaspoonfuls onto ungreased cookie sheets, 2 inches (5 cm) apart.

◆ Bake for 10 to 12 minutes. Cookies will be soft in centre when done. Cool 2 minutes; transfer to rack to cool.

Prep time: 10 minutes plus chilling
Baking time: 12 minutes
Makes about 4 dozen cookies.

ULTIMATE CHOCOLATE CHUNK COOKIES

1½ cups	butter or margarine, softened	375 mL
2 cups	packed brown sugar	500 mL
2	eggs	2
2 tsp	vanilla	10 mL
2 cups	all-purpose flour	500 mL
1 cup	whole wheat flour	250 mL
1 tsp	baking soda	5 mL
½ tsp	salt	2 mL
10	squares BAKER'S Bittersweet Chocolate, *each* square cut into 8 pieces	10
1 cup	coarsely chopped pecans	250 mL

◆ Heat oven to 375°F (190°C).

◆ Combine butter, brown sugar, eggs, and vanilla. Beat on low speed of electric mixer until well blended. Add flours, baking soda, and salt; blend well. Stir chocolate and nuts into batter.

◆ Drop from rounded tablespoonfuls onto ungreased cookie sheets.

◆ Bake for 8 to 10 minutes or until cookies are golden brown around the edges and appear slightly underbaked in the centre. Transfer to rack to cool.

Prep time: 20 minutes
Baking time: 10 minutes
Makes about 50 cookies.

CHOCO DUOS

Can't decide on what cookie to try?
Make these two cookies in one!

1½ cups	butter or margarine, softened	375 mL
1½ cups	packed brown sugar	375 mL
¾ cup	sugar	175 mL
3	eggs	3
3½ cups	all-purpose flour	875 mL
2 tsp	baking soda	10 mL
4	squares BAKER'S Bittersweet Chocolate, melted and cooled	4
1 pkg (225 g)	BAKER'S White Chocolate Chips	1 pkg (225 g)
½ cup	chopped pecans	125 mL
1 pkg (300 g)	BAKER'S Semi-Sweet Chocolate Chips	1 pkg (300 g)

◆ Heat oven to 350°F (180°C).

◆ Cream butter and sugars with mixer. Beat in eggs until fluffy. Mix in flour and baking soda by hand.

◆ Blend bittersweet chocolate, white chips and nuts into half of the batter. Stir semi-sweet chips into remaining batter in a separate bowl.

◆ Drop a teaspoonful of each batter side by side to make one cookie onto ungreased cookie sheets. Bake for 8 to 10 minutes until lightly browned.

Prep time: 25 minutes
Baking time: 10 minutes
Makes 5 dozen.

1

Beat butter with sugar and eggs.

2

Beat in melted chocolate.

3

Beat in remaining ingredients.

White Chocolate Apricot Biscotti

The Italian 'dunking' cookies, all the rage right now,
are baked twice to give them their characteristic crunch!

½ cup	butter or margarine	125 mL
1½ cups	sugar	375 mL
2	eggs	2
3	squares BAKER'S White Chocolate, melted and cooled	3
2¾ cups	all-purpose flour	675 mL
2½ tsp	baking powder	12 mL
1 tsp	salt	5 mL
¼ cup	orange juice	50 mL
1 tsp	almond extract	5 mL
3	squares BAKER'S White Chocolate, chopped	3
¾ cup	*each* coarsely chopped, toasted whole almonds and dried apricots	175 mL
	BAKER'S White and/or Bittersweet Chocolate (optional)	

◆ Heat oven to 350°F (180°C). Grease and flour two cookie sheets.

◆ Beat butter with sugar and eggs. Beat in melted chocolate.

◆ Add remaining ingredients, beating until well blended. Dough will be sticky.

◆ Spoon half of the dough onto each cookie sheet, shaping each into a long log, about 2 inches (5 cm) wide.

◆ Bake for 30 minutes, or until golden. Cool 10 minutes. Cut logs into ¾ inch (2 cm) wide slices.

◆ Place slices onto cookie sheets. Return to oven and bake 20 minutes longer, turning cookies over once during baking. Cool completely. If desired, dip cookies in melted white and/or bittersweet chocolate. Store in airtight container.

Prep time: 20 minutes
Baking time: 50 minutes
Makes about 40 cookies.

Note: Can be prepared two weeks ahead. Cookies will keep for 3 months in freezer.

Shape dough into two logs on cookie sheets.

Cut baked logs into slices and return to oven to bake once more.

PEANUT BUTTER CHOCOLATE BALLS

Peanut butter dunked in rich chocolate.

½ cup	chopped dates	125 mL
½ cup	chopped pecans	125 mL
1 cup	icing sugar, sifted	250 mL
½ cup	KRAFT Chunky Peanut Butter	125 mL
2 Tbsp	butter or margarine, melted	30 mL
6	squares BAKER'S Semi-Sweet Chocolate, chopped	6

◆ Combine dates, pecans, icing sugar, peanut butter and butter; mix well. Shape into 1 inch (2.5 cm) balls.

◆ Partially melt chocolate over hot water. Remove from heat and continue stirring until melted and smooth.

◆ Dip each ball in chocolate. Place on wax paper-lined baking sheet. Chill until firm. Store in refrigerator.

Prep time: 25 minutes plus chilling
Makes about 30 balls.

CHOCOLATE CHUBBIES

A chewy brownie cookie chock full of nuts.

8	squares Baker's Semi-Sweet Chocolate	8
3	squares Baker's Unsweetened Chocolate	3
½ cup	butter or margarine	125 mL
3	eggs	3
1¼ cups	sugar	300 mL
2 tsp	vanilla	10 mL
⅔ cup	all-purpose flour	150 mL
½ tsp	baking powder	2 mL
¼ tsp	salt	1 mL
1 pkg (300 g)	Baker's Semi-Sweet Chocolate Chips	1 pkg (300 g)
3 cups	chopped toasted nuts (pecans and walnuts)	750 mL

◆ Heat oven to 325°F (160°C).

◆ Melt chocolate with butter over low heat or in microwave on MEDIUM power for 3 minutes. Stir until smooth; let cool.

◆ Beat eggs with sugar until thick, about 5 minutes. Beat in chocolate mixture and vanilla.

◆ Stir in flour, baking powder, salt, chocolate chips and nuts.

◆ Drop batter by heaping tablespoonful onto greased cookie sheets.

◆ Bake for 10 minutes or until slightly cracked but moist. Let cool for 2 minutes; transfer cookies to rack to cool completely.

Prep time: 20 minutes
Baking time: 10 minutes
Makes about 30 cookies.

ALMOND CHOCOLATE BARS

Crust

¾ cup	all-purpose flour	175 mL
⅓ cup	icing sugar, sifted	75 mL
¼ cup	butter or margarine	50 mL
¼ tsp	almond extract	1 mL
1	egg yolk	1

Filling

1 cup	whole natural almonds	250 mL
½ cup	butter or margarine, softened	125 mL
¾ cup	sugar	175 mL
1 tsp	vanilla	5 mL
3	eggs	3
2 Tbsp	all-purpose flour	30 mL
½ tsp	cinnamon	2 mL
¼ tsp	nutmeg	1 mL

Glaze

3	squares BAKER'S Semi-Sweet Chocolate, chopped	3
1 Tbsp	butter	15 mL
	Whole natural almonds (optional)	

Crust:

◆ Heat oven to 350°F (180°C).

◆ Combine flour and icing sugar. Cut in butter until mixture resembles coarse crumbs. Stir in almond extract and egg yolk. Press firmly over bottom of lightly greased 8 inch (20 cm) square pan.

◆ Bake for 12 minutes or until lightly browned. Cool.

Filling:

◆ Spread nuts in shallow baking pan. Bake for 10 minutes, or until nuts are golden beneath the skins. Cool. Chop nuts in food processor until finely ground. Set aside.

◆ Cream butter. Gradually add sugar and continue beating until light and fluffy. Add vanilla and ground nuts. Add eggs, one at a time, beating well after each addition.

◆ Stir in flour, cinnamon and nutmeg; mix well. Spread filling mixture evenly over baked crust. Bake for 30 to 35 minutes or until cake tester inserted in centre comes out clean. Cool on rack.

Glaze:

◆ Partially melt chocolate and butter over low heat. Remove from heat and continue stirring until completely melted. Spread over filling. Chill. Cut into bars and decorate with whole almonds, if desired. Store in airtight container.

Prep time: 30 minutes
Baking time: 35 minutes
Makes about 32 bars.

TOFFEE CHOCOLATE CHIP BARS

The ultimate yet easy cookie bar.

1 cup	butter or margarine, softened	250 mL
1½ cups	packed brown sugar	375 mL
2	eggs	2
1 tsp	vanilla	5 mL
2 cups	all-purpose flour	500 mL
1 tsp	baking soda	5 mL
1 tsp	salt	5 mL
1 pkg (300 g)	BAKER'S Butterscotch Chips*	1 pkg (300 g)
4	squares BAKER'S Semi-Sweet Chocolate, each square cut into 8 pieces	4
½ cup	chopped pecans	125 mL

* Or substitute 1 pkg (300 g) BAKER'S Semi-Sweet Chocolate Chips

- ◆ Heat oven to 350°F (180°C).
- ◆ Beat butter, sugar, eggs and vanilla in large bowl until light and fluffy.
- ◆ Stir in flour, baking soda and salt until well blended. Stir in chips. Spread in greased 13 × 9 inch (33 × 23 cm) cake pan.
- ◆ Bake for 35 to 40 minutes or until cake tester inserted into centre comes out clean.
- ◆ Sprinkle chocolate over top; return to oven for 1 minute or until chocolate is melted. Spread chocolate evenly over surface then sprinkle with pecans. Cool; cut into bars.

Prep time: 20 minutes
Baking time: 40 minutes
Makes about 36 bars.

CHERRY JEWEL BARS

1¼ cups	all-purpose flour	300 mL
⅔ cup	packed brown sugar, divided	150 mL
¾ cup	butter or margarine	175 mL
1	egg	1
½ cup	salted peanuts	125 mL
½ cup	whole natural almonds	125 mL
½ cup	pecan halves	125 mL
1½ cups	mixed green and red candied cherries, halved	375 mL
1 cup	BAKERS Semi-Sweet Chocolate Chips	250 mL

- ◆ Heat oven to 350°F (180°C).
- ◆ Combine flour and ⅓ cup (75 mL) of the brown sugar. Blend in butter. Press mixture evenly into ungreased 15 × 10 inch (40 × 25 cm) jelly roll pan.
- ◆ Bake for 15 minutes.
- ◆ Beat egg and remaining brown sugar. Add nuts, cherries and chips. Mix well. Spoon mixture evenly over baked layer. Bake an additional 20 minutes. Cool, cut into bars.

Prep time: 20 minutes
Baking time: 35 minutes
Makes about 40 bars.

SACHER BARS

¾ cup	butter or margarine	175 mL
3	squares BAKER'S Unsweetened Chocolate	3
1½ cups	sugar	375 mL
3	eggs	3
1¼ cups	all-purpose flour	300 mL
1½ tsp	vanilla	7 mL
¾ cup	apricot jam	175 mL
2	squares BAKER'S Bittersweet Chocolate, melted	2

◆ Heat oven to 325°F (160°C).

◆ Melt butter and unsweetened chocolate over low heat. Remove from heat; stir in sugar. Cool slightly.

◆ Add eggs, one at a time, blending well after each addition. Add flour and vanilla; mix well. Spread evenly in greased and floured wax paper-lined 15 × 10 inch (40 × 25 cm) jelly roll pan.

◆ Bake 15 to 20 minutes or until toothpick inserted in centre comes out clean. Do not overbake. Cool.

◆ Heat jam over low heat. Strain jam through sieve to remove fruit pieces. Spread jam evenly over surface.

◆ Cut in half lengthwise then crosswise to make 4 rectangles. Stack 2 rectangles together, jam side up. Drizzle melted chocolate evenly over rectangles. Cut into bars. Store in airtight container in refrigerator.

Prep time: 30 minutes
Baking time: 20 minutes
Makes 40 bars.

DIXIE BARS

Base

1¼ cups	all-purpose flour	300 mL
¼ cup	sugar	50 mL
½ cup	butter or margarine	125 mL

Filling

1 can (300 mL)	sweetened condensed milk	1 can (300 mL)
½ cup	sugar	125 mL
½ cup	butter or margarine	125 mL
2 Tbsp	corn syrup	30 mL
1 cup	pecan pieces	250 mL

Topping

4	squares BAKER'S Semi-Sweet Chocolate, chopped	4
1 Tbsp	butter	15 mL
24	pecan halves	24

Base:

◆ Heat oven to 350°F (180°C).

◆ Combine flour and sugar; cut in butter to form a soft dough. Press evenly into an 8 inch (20 cm) square pan. Bake for 20 to 30 minutes or until golden brown.

Filling:

◆ Combine milk, sugar, butter and corn syrup in heavy saucepan, cook and stir over low heat until sugar is dissolved, about 5 minutes. Bring to a boil over medium-low heat and boil for 6 to 8 minutes, *stirring constantly* or until mixture thickens slightly and turns a caramel colour. Remove from heat; stir in pecan pieces. Spread evenly over base. Chill.

Topping:

◆ Partially melt chocolate with butter over low heat. Remove from heat and continue stirring until completely melted. Spread over caramel layer. Garnish with pecan halves.

Prep time: 20 minutes plus chilling
Baking time: 30 minutes
Makes 24 bars.

CHOCOLATE CARAMEL BARS

*Crumb layers sandwiching a chocolate
and chewy caramel middle.*

1 bag (198 g)	KRAFT Caramels (about 24)	1 bag (198 g)
½ cup	evaporated milk	125 mL
1 cup	all-purpose flour	250 mL
1 cup	quick-cooking rolled oats	250 mL
¾ cup	packed brown sugar	175 mL
½ tsp	baking soda	2 mL
¼ tsp	salt	1 mL
¾ cup	butter or margarine, softened	175 mL
1 cup	BAKER'S Semi-Sweet Chocolate Chips	250 mL
½ cup	chopped walnuts or pecans	125 mL

◆ Heat oven to 350°F (180°C).

◆ Melt caramels and evaporated milk on low heat or microwave on MEDIUM power for 5 minutes, stirring until smooth.

◆ Combine flour, oats, brown sugar, baking soda and salt in large mixing bowl. Cut in butter until mixture is crumbly. Press half of mixture into 9 inch (23 cm) square cake pan.

◆ Bake for 10 minutes.

◆ Sprinkle chocolate chips and walnuts evenly over baked crust. Pour caramel mixture on top. Sprinkle with remaining crumb mixture.

◆ Bake 20 to 25 minutes longer, or until golden. Cool; cut into bars.

Prep time: 20 minutes
Baking time: 35 minutes
Makes 24 bars.

CHOCOLATE RAISIN CHEWS

½ cup	butter or margarine	125 mL
1½ cups	graham crumbs	375 mL
1½ cups	raisins	375 mL
1 cup	coarsely chopped nuts	250 mL
1½ cups	BAKER'S ANGEL FLAKE Coconut	375 mL
1 can (300 mL)	sweetened condensed milk	1can (300 mL)
3	squares BAKER'S Semi-Sweet Chocolate, chopped	3
1 Tbsp	butter or margarine	15 mL

◆ Heat oven to 350°F (180°C).

◆ Place ½ cup (125 mL) butter in 13 × 9 inch (33 × 23 cm) pan in oven until melted.

◆ Remove from oven and stir in crumbs. Press down evenly to cover bottom of pan.

◆ Sprinkle with raisins, nuts and coconut; drizzle condensed milk evenly over surface. Bake for 25 to 30 minutes or until golden brown. Cool.

◆ Melt chocolate with remaining butter over low heat or in microwave on MEDIUM power 2 minutes. With a small spoon, drizzle over surface of bars. Chill.

Prep time: 20 minutes plus chilling
Baking time: 30 minutes
Makes about 36 bars.

BLACK BOTTOM COCONUT DREAM BARS

Crust

1¼ cups	all-purpose flour	300 mL
¼ cup	packed brown sugar	50 mL
½ cup	butter or margarine	125 mL
2	squares BAKER'S Unsweetened Chocolate, melted	2

Filling

2	eggs	2
1 cup	packed brown sugar	250 mL
¼ cup	all-purpose flour	50 mL
½ tsp	baking powder	2 mL
1⅓ cups	BAKER'S ANGEL FLAKE Coconut	325 mL
1 cup	BAKER'S Butterscotch *or* Semi-Sweet Chocolate Chips	250 mL
½ cup	chopped walnuts	125 mL
1 tsp	vanilla	5 mL

Crust:

◆ Heat oven to 350°F (180°C).

◆ Combine flour and sugar. Add butter and chocolate; mix until blended.

◆ Press into ungreased 9 inch (23 cm) square pan. Bake for 15 minutes.

Filling:

◆ Beat eggs until thick and light in colour. Gradually beat in sugar and continue beating until mixture is light and fluffy.

◆ Mix flour with baking powder; fold into egg mixture.

◆ Stir in coconut, chips, nuts and vanilla. Spread over baked crust in pan.

◆ Bake 20 to 25 minutes longer or until lightly browned. Cool; cut in bars.

Prep time: 30 minutes
Baking time: 40 minutes
Makes about 24 bars.

EXTRA CHOCOLATEY BANANA MUFFINS

⅓ cup	vegetable oil	75 mL
½ cup	sugar	125 mL
1	egg	1
1 cup	mashed ripe bananas (about 3 medium)	250 mL
1 pkg (300 g)	BAKER'S Semi-Sweet Chocolate Chips	1 pkg (300 g)
1 cup	all-purpose flour	250 mL
1 tsp	baking soda	5 mL
½ tsp	salt	2 mL
½ tsp	cinnamon	2 mL

◆ Heat oven to 350°F (180°C).

◆ Whisk together oil, sugar and egg; stir in bananas and half the package of chips.

◆ Combine flour, soda, salt and cinnamon; stir into mixture just to moisten.

◆ Spoon into 12 greased muffin cups. Sprinkle remaining chips evenly over top. Bake 15 to 20 minutes.

Prep time: 15 minutes
Baking time: 20 minutes
Makes 12 muffins.

CHOCOLATE PEANUT BUTTER TARTS

A Canadian tradition with a chocolate peanut butter twist.

3	squares BAKER'S Semi-Sweet Chocolate, coarsely chopped	3
12	unbaked medium tart shells	12
⅓ cup	corn syrup	75 mL
¼ cup	KRAFT Smooth Peanut Butter	50 mL
¼ cup	sugar	50 mL
½ tsp	vanilla	2 mL
2	eggs	2

◆ Heat oven to 400°F (200°C).

◆ Place chocolate pieces in bottom of tart shells.

◆ Stir together remaining ingredients until smooth. Pour over chocolate to fill shells.

◆ Bake on bottom rack of oven, 12 to 15 minutes.

Prep time: 15 minutes
Baking time: 15 minutes
Makes 12 servings.

Note: Recipe may also be made using 24 small tart shells. Bake 10 to 13 minutes.

1

Beat flour and sugar into creamed butter until crumbly.

2

Add next five ingredients to flour mixture and stir to blend and moisten ingredients.

3

Spread one third of batter into pan.

Pear Coffeecake Belle-Hélène

¾ cup	butter or margarine, softened	175 mL
2½ cups	all-purpose flour	625 mL
1 cup	sugar	250 mL
½ tsp	baking powder	2 mL
½ tsp	baking soda	2 mL
4	squares BAKER'S Unsweetened Chocolate, melted	4
1	egg, beaten	1
1 cup	milk	250 mL
1 can (28 oz)	pear halves, well drained	1 can (796 mL)
⅓ cup	pecan halves	75 mL

◆ Heat oven to 350°F (180°C).

◆ Beat butter with electric mixer until creamy. Add flour and sugar, beating on low speed until crumbly. Remove ⅓ cup (75 mL); set aside.

◆ Add baking powder, baking soda, chocolate, egg and milk to remaining mixture in bowl. Stir just to blend and moisten ingredients.

◆ Spread one-third of the batter in a greased 9 inch (23 cm) springform pan. Place pear halves, cut side down, in a circular pattern over batter. Drop spoonfuls of remaining batter over pears and spread evenly. Sprinkle with reserved crumb mixture and pecans.

◆ Bake for 70 minutes or until toothpick inserted in centre comes out clean. Cool.

Prep time: 20 minutes
Baking time: 70 minutes
Makes 8 servings.

4

Place pears on top of batter.

5

Drop spoonfuls of remaining batter over pears and spread evenly.

6

Sprinkle with reserved crumb mixture and pecans.

Banana Chip Coffee Cake

A moist chocolate banana cake with a touch of cinnamon.

1 cup	butter or margarine, softened	250 mL
2 cups	sugar	500 mL
2	eggs, beaten	2
1 tsp	vanilla	5 mL
2½ cups	mashed ripe bananas (about 7 medium)	625 mL
3 cups	all-purpose flour	750 mL
2 tsp	baking powder	10 mL
2 tsp	baking soda	10 mL
1 cup	sour cream	250 mL
1 tsp	cinnamon	5 mL
½ cup	packed brown sugar	125 mL
1 pkg (300 g)	BAKER'S Semi-Sweet Chocolate Chips	1 pkg (300 g)

◆ Heat oven to 350°F (180°C).

◆ Beat together butter and sugar. Add beaten eggs and beat until smooth. Add vanilla and mashed bananas; mix until smooth.

◆ Combine flour, baking powder and baking soda. Add to banana mixture alternately with sour cream, ending with dry ingredients.

◆ Pour half the batter into a greased 9 × 13 inch (23 × 33 cm) pan.

◆ Combine cinnamon and brown sugar. Sprinkle half of the mixture over the batter in pan. Top with half of the chocolate chips. Repeat layers. Bake for 45 to 50 minutes or until toothpick inserted in centre comes out clean. Cool in pan.

Prep time: 20 minutes
Baking time: 50 minutes
Makes 12 servings.

Chocolate Zucchini Cake

Zucchini makes this cake ultra moist.

2	squares BAKER'S Unsweetened Chocolate, melted and cooled	2
1½ cups	all-purpose flour	375 mL
1½ cups	sugar	375 mL
¾ cup	vegetable oil	175 mL
2	eggs	2
¾ tsp	baking powder	4 mL
½ tsp	baking soda	2 mL
½ tsp	salt	2 mL
1½ cups	grated zucchini	375 mL
½ cup	coarsely chopped nuts	125 mL
	Icing sugar (optional)	

◆ Heat oven to 350°F (180°C).

◆ Combine chocolate, flour, sugar, oil, eggs, baking powder, baking soda and salt. Mix with fork for 2 minutes or until smooth. Blend in zucchini and nuts.

◆ Spoon into 8 inch (20 cm) square baking pan.

◆ Bake for 45 minutes or until toothpick inserted in centre comes out clean. Cool. Sprinkle with icing sugar, if desired.

Prep time: 15 minutes
Baking time: 45 minutes
Makes 9 servings.

Banana Chip Coffee Cake

ORANGE CHOCOLATE SWIRL LOAF

Fresh zest of orange and chocolate marble this light loaf.

Cake

1¼ cups	all-purpose flour	300 mL
½ tsp	baking soda	2 mL
½ tsp	salt	2 mL
½ cup	butter or margarine, softened	125 mL
1 cup	packed brown sugar	250 mL
3	eggs	3
½ cup	sour cream	125 mL
4	squares BAKER'S Semi-Sweet Chocolate, melted and cooled	4
1 Tbsp	grated orange zest	15 mL

Glaze

3	squares BAKER'S Semi-Sweet Chocolate	3
1½ Tbsp	butter	25 mL
1½ Tbsp	orange juice	25 mL
½ tsp	vegetable oil	2 mL

Cake:

- ◆ Heat oven to 350°F (180°C).
- ◆ Combine flour, baking soda, and salt.
- ◆ Cream butter and sugar until light and fluffy. Beat in eggs, one at a time, until well blended.
- ◆ Alternately blend in flour mixture and sour cream, one-third at a time on low speed of electric mixer. Measure 1 cup (250 mL) batter; add chocolate and mix well. Blend orange rind into remaining batter; mix well.
- ◆ Layer half of orange batter into greased and floured 9 × 5 inch (23 × 13 cm) loaf pan. Spread with chocolate batter. Top with spoonfuls of remaining orange batter. Draw knife through layers to marble.
- ◆ Bake for 1 hour or until toothpick inserted in centre comes out clean. Cool in pan for 10 minutes; remove and finish cooling on rack.

Glaze:

- ◆ Melt chocolate with butter, orange juice and oil over low heat. Blend until smooth. Spread evenly over entire loaf.

Prep time: 30 minutes
Baking time: 1 hour
Makes 10 servings.

CHOCOLATE FLECK COFFEE CAKE

Cake

2 cups	all-purpose flour	500 mL
½ tsp	baking powder	2 mL
¼ tsp	salt	1 mL
1 cup	sour cream	250 mL
1 tsp	baking soda	5 mL
½ cup	butter or margarine, softened	125 mL
1 cup	sugar	250 mL
2	eggs	2
½ tsp	vanilla	2 mL
3	squares BAKER'S Semi-Sweet Chocolate, coarsely grated	3

Topping

⅓ cup	bran flake cereal	75 mL
⅓ cup	packed brown sugar	75 mL
½ tsp	cinnamon	2 mL
2	squares BAKER'S Semi-Sweet Chocolate	2
2 tsp	butter	10 mL

Cake:

◆ Heat oven to 350°F (180°C).

◆ Combine flour, baking powder, salt; set aside. Combine sour cream and baking soda. Set aside.

◆ Beat butter with sugar until light and fluffy. Add eggs, one at a time, beating well after each addition. Add vanilla.

◆ Alternately blend in flour mixture and sour cream, one third at a time, with electric mixer. Fold in grated chocolate.

◆ Pour into greased and floured 9 inch (23 cm) square pan.

Topping:

◆ Combine cereal, brown sugar and cinnamon; mix well. Sprinkle evenly over surface of batter.

◆ Bake for 45 to 50 minutes, or until toothpick inserted in centre comes out clean. Cool in pan on wire rack.

◆ Partially melt chocolate with butter over low heat. With a small spoon, drizzle over topping.

Prep time: 30 minutes
Baking time: 50 minutes
Makes 12 servings.

Beat butter with sugar until light and fluffy.

Beat in eggs one at a time.

Alternately blend in flour mixture and sour cream.

4

Alternately blend in flour
mixture and sour cream.

5

Fold in grated chocolate.

6

Sprinkle cereal mixture over
surface of batter.

BANANA CHOCOLATE CHUNK BREAD

2	eggs, lightly beaten	2
1 cup	mashed ripe bananas (about 3 medium)	250 mL
⅓ cup	vegetable oil	75 mL
¼ cup	milk	50 mL
2 cups	all-purpose flour	500 mL
1 cup	sugar	250 mL
2 tsp	baking powder	10 mL
¼ tsp	salt	1 mL
8	squares BAKER'S Semi-Sweet Chocolate, coarsely chopped	8
½ cup	chopped nuts	125 mL
¼ cup	packed brown sugar	50 mL
½ tsp	cinnamon	2 mL

◆ Heat oven to 350°F (180°C).

◆ Stir eggs, banana, oil and milk until well blended.

◆ Add flour, sugar, baking powder and salt; stir just until moistened. Stir in chocolate and nuts.

◆ Pour into greased 9 × 5 inch (23 × 13 cm) loaf pan.

◆ Combine brown sugar and cinnamon. Sprinkle on top of batter.

◆ Bake for 60 minutes or until toothpick inserted in centre comes out clean. Cool 10 minutes. Remove from pan; finish cooling on rack.

Prep time: 10 minutes
Baking time: 60 minutes
Makes 14 servings.

Everyday Desserts

1

Melt oil and chocolate in pan in oven.

2

Beat in next ingredients with fork until smooth.

3

Stir in half the chips.

MIX EASY DOUBLE CHOCOLATE CAKE

Our easiest mix-in-the-pan extra moist chocolate cake.

⅓ cup	vegetable oil	75 mL
2	squares BAKER'S Unsweetened Chocolate	2
¾ cup	water	175 mL
1 cup	sugar	250 mL
1	egg	1
1¼ cups	all-purpose flour	300 mL
½ tsp	salt	2 mL
½ tsp	baking soda	2 mL
1 tsp	vanilla	5 mL
1 pkg (300 g)	BAKER'S Semi-Sweet Chocolate Chips	1 pkg (300 g)
⅓ cup	chopped nuts	75 mL

◆ Heat oven to 350°F (180°C).

◆ Heat oil and chocolate in an 8 inch (20 cm) square cake pan in oven for about 4 minutes, until melted.

◆ Add water, sugar, egg, flour, salt, baking soda and vanilla. Beat with a fork until smooth, about 2 minutes. Stir in half of the chips.

◆ Spread batter evenly in pan. Sprinkle batter with nuts and remaining chocolate chips.

◆ Bake for 40 minutes. Cool.

Prep time: 10 minutes
Baking time: 40 minutes
Makes 9 servings.

4

Sprinkle batter with nuts and remaining chips.

OLD-FASHIONED BROWNIE PUDDING

Pudding		
2	squares BAKER'S Unsweetened Chocolate	2
¼ cup	butter or margarine	50 mL
1 cup	all-purpose flour	250 mL
½ tsp	baking powder	2 mL
½ tsp	salt	2 mL
⅔ cup	sugar	150 mL
½ cup	milk	125 mL
1 tsp	vanilla	5 mL
½ cup	chopped nuts	125 mL
Sauce		
1¾ cups	cold water	425 mL
1 tsp	cornstarch	5 mL
2	squares BAKER'S Unsweetened Chocolate, chopped	2
½ cup	packed brown sugar	125 mL
¼ cup	sugar	50 mL
	Ice cream	

Pudding:

◆ Heat oven to 350°F (180°C).

◆ Melt 2 squares chocolate and butter in 8 inch (20 cm) square pan for about 5 minutes.

◆ Add flour, baking powder, salt, sugar, milk, and vanilla. Beat with fork until smooth and creamy, about 2 minutes. Stir in nuts. Spread evenly in pan.

Sauce:

◆ Combine cold water and cornstarch in saucepan; mix well. Add 2 squares chocolate and sugars.

◆ Bring to a boil over medium heat, stirring constantly. Remove from heat and pour over cake in pan.

◆ Bake for 45 to 50 minutes or until sauce bubbles and cake begins to pull away from sides of pan. Serve warm, topped with a scoop of ice cream.

Prep time: 20 minutes
Baking time: 50 minutes
Makes 6 servings

CHOCOLATE CRATER PIE

½ cup	butter or margarine	125 mL
2	squares BAKER'S Unsweetened Chocolate, chopped	2
1	square BAKER'S Semi-Sweet Chocolate, chopped	1
3	eggs	3
1⅓ cups	sugar	325 mL
3 Tbsp	corn syrup	45 mL
2 Tbsp	sour cream	30 mL
1 Tbsp	instant coffee granules	15 mL
1½ tsp	vanilla	7 mL
1	9 inch (23 cm) unbaked pie shell	1
	Plain or coffee-flavoured whipped cream or ice cream (optional)	

◆ Heat oven to 350°F (180°C).

◆ Melt butter and chocolate together over low heat or in microwave on MEDIUM power 2 minutes. Set aside.

◆ Combine eggs, sugar, syrup, sour cream, coffee and vanilla. Mix well. Stir in chocolate mixture. Pour into prepared pie shell.

◆ Bake on bottom rack for 40 to 50 minutes or until filling is set, puffed up and starting to crack on top. Cool to room temperature. Serve with whipped cream or ice cream, if desired.

Prep time: 15 minutes
Baking time: 50 minutes
Makes about 8 servings.

Helpful Hint: Don't be alarmed at the unique appearance of this pie. The filling is supposed to rise up and crack during baking and sink slightly on cooling.

MIRACLE WHIP FUDGE CAKE

Cake

1½ cups	MIRACLE WHIP Salad Dressing	375 mL
2¼ cups	packed brown sugar	550 mL
1½ tsp	vanilla	7 mL
3	eggs	3
6	squares BAKER'S Unsweetened Chocolate, melted, cooled	6
2¼ cups	cake and pastry flour	550 mL
2 tsp	baking soda	10 mL
½ tsp	salt	2 mL
1 cup	boiling water	250 mL

Icing

4	squares BAKER'S Unsweetened Chocolate	4
½ cup	butter or margarine	125 mL
3½ cups	icing sugar, sifted	875 mL
½ cup	milk	125 mL
1 tsp	vanilla	5 mL

Cake:

◆ Heat oven to 350°F (180°C).

◆ Combine salad dressing, sugar and vanilla with electric mixer. Blend in eggs and chocolate.

◆ Add combined dry ingredients alternately with water, mixing well after each addition.

◆ Pour into 2 wax paper-lined 9 inch (23 cm) round cake pans. Bake 30 to 35 minutes or until toothpick inserted in centre comes out clean. Cool 10 minutes; remove from pans. Cool completely.

Icing:

◆ Melt chocolate and butter over low heat. Cool to lukewarm. Beat in sugar, milk and vanilla with electric mixer until smooth. Chill until icing is of spreading consistency.

◆ Spread 1 cup (250 mL) icing between layers and remaining icing over top and sides of cake.

Prep time: 20 minutes
Baking time: 35 minutes
Makes 10 to 12 servings.

CHOCOLATE BREAD PUDDING
WITH WHITE CHOCOLATE CUSTARD SAUCE

Pudding

2½ cups	light (18% b.f.) cream or milk	625 mL
6	squares BAKER'S Semi-Sweet Chocolate, chopped	6
3	eggs	3
3	egg yolks	3
½ cup	sugar	125 mL
8 cups	egg bread, cubed (about 8 slices)	2 L

Pudding:

◆ Heat chocolate and cream in heavy saucepan over low heat until melted and smooth.

◆ Whisk together eggs, yolks and sugar; stir in chocolate mixture.

◆ Arrange bread in 9 inch (23 cm) square pan; pour chocolate mixture over bread. Let stand 30 minutes.

◆ Heat oven to 325°F (160°C). Cover pan with foil and puncture with fork for steam vents. Place pan in larger shallow baking dish. Pour in enough boiling water to reach halfway up sides of pan.

◆ Bake for 65 to 75 minutes, or until set. Let cool for at least 30 minutes before serving. Cut into squares and serve with Custard Sauce.

Custard Sauce:

◆ In microwaveable bowl, beat together 2 egg yolks, ¼ cup (50 mL) sugar and 1 tsp (5 mL) cornstarch until light. In glass measure heat 1 cup (250 mL) light cream on HIGH for about 2 minutes until hot; beat into yolk mixture.

◆ Microwave on HIGH until mixture starts to boil, about 2 minutes, stirring once. Stir in 3 squares chopped BAKER'S White Chocolate until melted and smooth.

Prep time: 30 minutes
Baking time: 75 minutes
Makes about 9 servings.

Ice Cream Squares

*A make-ahead frozen treat – they'll think you have
your own ice cream parlour.*

	Chocolate Satin Sauce (see page 184)	
20	**chocolate sandwich wafer cookies, crushed**	20
1 (2 L)	**container vanilla ice cream, softened**	1 (2L)
½ cup	**chopped peanuts**	125 mL

◆ Prepare chocolate sauce. Let cool 20 minutes.

◆ Press crushed cookies onto bottom of a wax paper-lined 9 inch (23 cm) square pan.

◆ Spoon half of vanilla ice cream over cookie crust. Drizzle with one-third of chocolate sauce and sprinkle with half of the peanuts.

◆ Spoon remaining ice cream on top, smooth surface. Cover with remaining chocolate sauce; sprinkle with remaining peanuts.

◆ Freeze until firm, about 3 hours. Cut into squares and serve.

*Prep time: 30 minutes plus freezing
Makes 9 servings.*

1

Beat chocolate, eggs and vanilla into butter mixture.

2

Mix in dry ingredients alternately with milk.

3

Mix in dry ingredients alternately with milk.

GERMAN CHOCOLATE CAKE

*Our most popular and enduring cake recipe
for Baker's Sweet Chocolate.*

Cake

1 cup	butter or margarine	250 mL
1⅔ cup	sugar	400 mL
4	eggs, separated	4
4	squares BAKER'S Sweet Chocolate, melted	4
1 tsp	vanilla	5 mL
2¼ cups	all-purpose flour	550 mL
2 tsp	baking powder	10 mL
½ tsp	salt	2 mL
1¼ cups	milk	300 mL

Topping

½ cup	butter or margarine	125 mL
½ cup	packed brown sugar	125 mL
½ cup	milk	125 mL
2	eggs	2
2 cups	chopped pecans	500 mL
2 cups	BAKER'S ANGEL FLAKE Coconut	500 mL
2 tsp	vanilla	10 mL

Cake:

◆ Heat oven to 350°F (180°C).

◆ Beat butter and sugar until light and fluffy; blend in egg yolks, chocolate and vanilla.

◆ Add combined dry ingredients alternately with milk, mixing well after each addition. Fold in stiffly beaten egg whites.

◆ Pour into three greased and floured 9 inch (23 cm) layer pans.

◆ Bake for 25 to 30 minutes or until toothpick inserted in centre comes out clean. Cool 10 minutes; remove from pans; cool.

Topping:

◆ Combine butter, sugar, milk and eggs in saucepan. Cook over low heat, stirring constantly, until thickened. Stir in remaining ingredients.

◆ Evenly spread each layer with one-third of topping. Stack layers one on top of the other. Cover and store in refrigerator.

*Prep time: 20 minutes plus cooling
Baking time: 30 minutes
Makes 12 servings.*

Fold egg whites into batter.

Prepare topping.

Spread topping over layers and stack layers.

Busy Day Chocolate Apricot Flan

¾ cup	all-purpose flour	175 mL
¾ cup	sugar	175 mL
2 tsp	baking powder	10 mL
¼ tsp	salt	1 mL
3	squares BAKER'S Unsweetened Chocolate, melted	3
½ cup	butter or margarine, melted	125 mL
½ cup	milk	125 mL
2	eggs	2
1 tsp	vanilla	5 mL
2 Tbsp	liqueur	30 mL
1 can (14 oz)	apricots halves, drained	1 can (398 mL)
2 Tbsp	apricot jam	30 mL
2	squares BAKER'S Semi-Sweet Chocolate, grated	2

◆ Heat oven to 375°F (190°C).

◆ Combine first 9 ingredients in large bowl. Blend on low speed with electric mixer for 1 minute. Pour into a greased 9½ inch (24 cm) flan pan with removeable bottom.

◆ Bake for 20 to 25 minutes or until toothpick inserted in centre comes out clean. Cool in pan on rack; remove cake from pan.

◆ Brush 1 Tbsp (15 mL) of liqueur onto surface of cake. Top with apricot halves, cut side down.

◆ Melt apricot jam with remaining liqueur over medium heat, 1 to 2 minutes.

◆ Brush glaze over top of cake and apricots. Sprinkle with grated chocolate.

Prep time: 20 minutes
Baking time: 25 minutes
Makes 8 servings.

Birthdays and Celebrations

BAKER'S BEST BIRTHDAY CAKE

Cake

1¾ cups	all-purpose flour	425 mL
1¾ cups	sugar	425 mL
1¼ tsp	baking soda	6 mL
½ tsp	salt	2 mL
¼ tsp	baking powder	1 mL
⅔ cup	butter or margarine, softened	150 mL
4	squares BAKER'S Unsweetened Chocolate, melted and cooled	4
1¼ cups	water	300 mL
1 tsp	vanilla	5 mL
3	eggs	3

Icing

4	squares BAKER'S Unsweetened Chocolate	4
½ cup	butter or margarine, softened	125 mL
¼ cup	milk	50 mL
1	egg, slightly beaten	1
2½ cups	icing sugar, sifted	625 mL

Cake:

◆ Heat oven to 350° F (180° C).

◆ Combine cake ingredients except eggs. Beat at medium speed of electric mixer for 2 minutes. Add eggs, beat 2 minutes longer. Pour into greased and floured 9 inch (23 cm) cake pans.

◆ Bake for 35 to 40 minutes or until toothpick inserted in centre comes out clean. Cool in pans 10 minutes; remove from pans and cool on racks.

Icing:

◆ Melt chocolate with butter and milk over low heat until smooth; cool. Blend in egg. Add icing sugar, beat at medium speed 1 minute. Chill until spreadable.

To assemble:

◆ Spread 1 cup (250 mL) of icing on one layer. Top with second layer. Frost with remaining icing, decorate with chocolate cutouts.

Prep time: 60 minutes
Baking time: 40 minutes
Makes 10 servings.

FUN AND EASY TOP CUPCAKES

Cupcakes

6	squares BAKER'S Semi-Sweet Chocolate	6
¾ cup	butter or margarine	175 mL
1½ cups	sugar	375 mL
3	eggs	3
2 tsp	vanilla	10 mL
2½ cups	all-purpose flour	625 mL
1 tsp	baking soda	5 mL
½ tsp	salt	2 mL
1½ cups	water	375 mL

Icing

1 cup	COOL WHIP Whipped Topping, thawed	250 mL
3 (142 g each)	containers MAGIC MOMENTS Chocolate Pudding	3 (142 g each)
	KRAFT Miniature Marshmallows	
	BAKER'S Miniature Semi-Sweet Chocolate Chips	

Cupcakes:

◆ Heat oven to 350°F (180°C).

◆ Microwave chocolate and butter in large microwaveable bowl on HIGH for 2 minutes or until butter is melted. Stir until chocolate is completely melted.

◆ Stir sugar into melted chocolate mixture until well blended.

◆ Beat in eggs, one at a time, with electric mixer. Add vanilla.

◆ Stir in ½ cup (125 mL) flour, baking soda and salt. Beat in remaining flour alternately with water until well blended and smooth. Pour into 24 paper-lined muffin cups.

◆ Bake for 25 minutes or until toothpick inserted in centre comes out clean. Cool.

Icing:

◆ Stir whipped topping gently into pudding. Spoon icing over cupcakes. Decorate with miniature marshmallows and chocolate chips.

Prep time: 20 minutes
Baking time: 25 minutes
Makes 24 cupcakes.

CHOCOLATE DIPPED STRAWBERRIES

4	squares BAKER'S Semi-Sweet Chocolate	4
1 pint	strawberries	500 mL

◆ Partially melt chocolate over hot water. Remove from heat and continue stirring until melted and smooth.

◆ Wash strawberries and dry thoroughly; do not hull.

◆ Dip bottom half of each strawberry in chocolate. Place on waxed paper. Chill until chocolate is firm.

◆ Store any leftover strawberries in refrigerator. May be prepared 4 to 6 hours in advance.

Prep time: 15 minutes plus chilling
Makes about 12 strawberries.

CHOCOLATE STARSHIPS

Cupcakes

2	squares BAKER'S Unsweetened Chocolate, melted and cooled	2
⅓ cup	vegetable oil	75 mL
¾ cup	water	175 mL
1 cup	sugar	250 mL
1	egg	1
1¼ cups	all-purpose flour	300 mL
½ tsp	baking soda	2 mL
½ tsp	salt	2 mL
1 tsp	vanilla	5 mL

Icing

2	squares BAKER'S Unsweetened Chocolate	2
¼ cup	butter or margarine	50 mL
1⅓ cups	icing sugar, sifted	325 mL
¼ tsp	salt	1 mL
1	egg, well-beaten	1
1 tsp	vanilla	5 mL
	Icing sugar	
	Decorating candies	

Cupcakes:

◆ Heat oven to 350°F (180°C).

◆ Combine cupcake ingredients. Beat with fork until smooth and creamy, about 2 minutes.

◆ Pour into 12 foil or paper-lined muffin cups. Bake for 25 minutes or until toothpick inserted in centre comes out clean. Cool.

Icing:

◆ Melt chocolate and butter over low heat. Cool.

◆ Add sugar, salt, egg and vanilla; blend until smooth.

◆ Chill until of spreading consistency, about ½ hour.

◆ Cut rounded top off each cupcake; set aside. Spread about 2 Tbsp (30 mL) icing on cut surface. Cut tops in half, sprinkle with icing sugar and inset into icing. Decorate with candies.

Prep time: 30 minutes
Baking time: 25 minutes
Makes 12 cupcakes.

HEART OF MY HEART CAKE

Cake

½ cup	butter or margarine, softened	125 mL
1¼ cups	all-purpose flour	300 mL
1¼ cups	sugar	300 mL
¾ tsp	baking soda	3 mL
¾ tsp	salt	3 mL
⅔ cup	water	150 mL
2	squares BAKER'S Unsweetened Chocolate, melted and cooled	2
2	eggs	2
1 tsp	vanilla	5 mL

Icing

4	squares BAKER'S Unsweetened Chocolate, melted and cooled	4
½ cup	butter or margarine, softened	125 mL
¼ cup	milk	50 mL
1	egg, slightly beaten	1
2½ cups	icing sugar, sifted	625 mL

Chocolate Hearts

1	square BAKER'S Semi-Sweet Chocolate	1
	Icing sugar	

Cake:

◆ Heat oven to 350°F (180°C).

◆ Cream butter. Combine flour, sugar, baking soda and salt. Add flour mixture and water to butter. Blend, then beat at medium speed of mixer for 1 minute.

◆ Add chocolate, eggs, and vanilla. Beat on low speed of electric mixer for 1 minute. Pour into greased and floured 9 inch (23 cm) square pan.

◆ Bake for 45 minutes or until toothpick inserted in centre comes out clean. Cool in pan 10 minutes; remove and finish cooling on rack.

◆ Cut a piece of waxed paper into 8¼ inch (21 cm) square. Fold along diagonal; draw a half heart shape. Cut out. Unfold heart, place on cake and cut cake into heart shape.

◆ Ice, then garnish with chocolate hearts and icing sugar.

Icing:

◆ Melt chocolate with butter and milk over low heat; blend until smooth. Cool.

◆ Blend in egg. Add icing sugar; beat at medium speed 1 minute. Chill until of spreading consistency.

Chocolate Hearts:

◆ Partially melt 1 square BAKER'S Semi-Sweet Chocolate over hot water. Remove from heat and continue stirring until completely melted.

◆ Pour onto waxed paper. Cover with a second sheet of waxed paper and roll with rolling pin until ⅛ inch (0.3 cm) thick. Chill until firm, about 5 minutes. Peel off top layer of waxed paper and cut with heart shaped cookie cutter. If you find the chocolate too brittle, let stand at room temperature for a few minutes. Store in refrigerator.

Prep time: 1 hour
Baking time: 45 minutes
Makes 12 servings.

1

Brush apricot jam over cake.

2

Melt glaze ingredients in a bowl over hot water.

3

Pour glaze over cake and bang rack to smooth the surface.

BAKER'S BEST CELEBRATION CAKE

The perfect cake for celebrating an anniversary or special day –
add a sparkler and your dreams will come true.

Cake

4	squares BAKER'S Unsweetened Chocolate, chopped	4
¼ cup	butter or margarine	50 mL
1 cup	milk	250 mL
4	eggs, separated	4
2 cups	sugar	500 mL
1 cup	all-purpose flour	250 mL
1½ tsp	baking powder	7 mL
1 cup	apricot jam	250 mL

Glaze

4	squares BAKER'S Semi-Sweet *or* Bittersweet Chocolate, chopped	4
1½ Tbsp	butter	25 mL
2 Tbsp	apricot brandy	30 mL
½ tsp	vegetable oil	2 mL
	Chocolate curls	
	Icing sugar, sifted	

Cake:

◆ Heat oven to 350°F (180°C).

◆ Melt chocolate with butter and milk over low heat. Blend until smooth and slightly thickened; cool.

◆ Beat egg yolks. Gradually add sugar, mixing well. Stir in chocolate mixture. Fold in flour and baking powder until well blended.

◆ Beat egg whites until stiff peaks form. Fold chocolate mixture gently into egg whites. Pour into greased and floured 9 inch (23 cm) springform pan. Bake for 55 minutes. Cool on rack. Remove from pan. If surface cracks, peel off crust layer to make it smooth.

◆ Heat apricot jam just until boiling. Strain jam through sieve to remove fruit pieces. Brush over entire cake. Leave cake on rack over waxed paper.

Glaze:

◆ Melt chocolate with butter, brandy and oil over hot water, stirring until smooth.

◆ Pour glaze over entire cake. Bang rack several times to smooth and evenly coat cake. Garnish with chocolate curls and icing sugar.

Prep time: 50 minutes
Baking time: 55 minutes
Makes 12 servings.

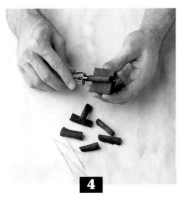

4

Make curls by shaving underside of a chocolate square with a vegetable peeler.

5

Decorate cake with curls and icing sugar.

FUDGE LOVER'S CAKE

Deep, dark ... and delicious!

Cake

3	eggs, separated	3
⅔ cup	butter or margarine, softened	150 mL
¾ cup	sugar	175 mL
5	squares BAKER'S Bittersweet Chocolate, melted	5
⅔ cup	all-purpose flour	150 mL
¼ cup	milk	50 mL
½ cup	ground almonds	125 mL
½ tsp	almond extract	2 mL

Icing

5	squares BAKER'S Bittersweet Chocolate	5
¼ cup	butter or margarine	50 mL
3 Tbsp	milk	45 mL
1 cup	sifted icing sugar	250 mL
¼ tsp	almond extract	1 mL

Garnish

½ cup	sliced almonds, toasted	125 mL

Cake:

◆ Heat oven to 350°F (180°C).

◆ Beat egg whites until stiff; set aside.

◆ Cream butter, adding sugar gradually. Beat in egg yolks and chocolate.

◆ Stir in flour and milk alternately until well blended. Stir in ground almonds and almond extract.

◆ Fold in egg whites just until combined.

◆ Spread batter in a greased 9 inch (23 cm) springform pan.

◆ Bake 35 to 40 minutes or until toothpick inserted in centre comes out clean. Cool 10 minutes before removing sides. Cool completely before icing.

Icing:

◆ Melt chocolate with butter and milk over low heat or in microwave on MEDIUM power for 2 to 3 minutes. Lightly whisk in icing sugar and almond extract until smooth. Spread on cake. Garnish sides with almonds.

Prep time: 30 minutes
Baking time: 40 minutes
Makes 12 servings.

CHOCOLATE CINNAMON TRUFFLE TORTE

Everyone will wonder how you made this...

Cake

½ cup	butter or margarine, softened	125 mL
¾ cup	sugar, divided	175 mL
1 tsp	vanilla	5 mL
7	eggs, separated	7
⅓ cup	all-purpose flour	75 mL
3 Tbsp	cornstarch	45 mL
2	squares BAKER'S Unsweetened Chocolate	2
1 Tbsp	vegetable oil	15 mL
½ tsp	cinnamon	2 mL

Glaze

4	squares BAKER'S Semi-Sweet *or* Bittersweet Chocolate, chopped	4
2 Tbsp	water	30 mL
2 Tbsp	butter or margarine	30 mL
	BAKER'S Semi-Sweet *or* Bittersweet & White Chocolate curls (optional)	

Cake:

◆ Beat butter, ¼ cup (50 mL) sugar and vanilla with electric mixer. Beat in egg yolks one at a time. Combine flour and cornstarch; stir into butter mixture. Divide batter in half.

◆ Melt chocolate with oil over low heat; stir chocolate into one half of batter and cinnamon into the other.

◆ Beat egg whites until soft peaks form. Gradually add remaining sugar, beating until stiff peaks form.

◆ Fold half the egg whites into each batter (batters may appear curdled).

◆ Grease and flour a 9 inch (23 cm) round pan.

◆ Spread ½ cup (125 mL) chocolate batter in pan. Place under preheated broiler about 5 inches (13 cm) from heat. Broil about 2 minutes, until baked. Repeat with cinnamon batter. Continue alternating until both batters are used up, about 10 layers. Cool cake on rack. Remove from pan.

Glaze:

◆ Melt chocolate, water and butter over low heat, stirring until smooth. Leave cake on rack over waxed paper; pour glaze over entire cake. Bang rack several times to smooth and evenly coat cake. If desired, garnish with chocolate curls. Serve at room temperature to ensure shiny glaze.

Prep time: 10 minutes
Baking time: 20 minutes
Makes 10 servings.

CHOCOLATE MACADAMIA NUT CAKE

Our most decadent chocolate cake!

Icing

½ cup	whipping cream	125 mL
2 Tbsp	butter or margarine	30 mL
6	squares BAKER'S Bittersweet Chocolate, broken in half	6

Chocolate Cake

½ cup	macadamia nuts, brazil nuts or hazelnuts	125 mL
¼ cup	butter or margarine	50 mL
½ cup	sugar	125 mL
4	eggs, separated	4
6	squares BAKER'S Bittersweet Chocolate, finely chopped	6
¼ cup	sour cream	50 mL
1 tsp	vanilla	5 mL
	Chocolate-dipped macadamia nuts	

Icing:

◆ Combine cream and butter in saucepan. Cook over low heat until butter is melted.

◆ Add chocolate to cream mixture; stir well until blended. Chill until of spreading consistency.

Chocolate Cake:

◆ Heat oven to 300°F (150°C).

◆ Grind nuts in food processor until coarsely chopped; remove and set aside.

◆ Bring butter and sugar to a boil over medium heat; boil 1 minute.

◆ Combine sugar mixture and egg yolks in processor. Add chocolate; blend until chocolate is melted. Add sour cream, vanilla and nuts; mix until blended.

◆ Beat egg whites until soft peaks form. Fold one-quarter of the egg whites into chocolate mixture. Fold in remaining egg whites.

◆ Pour batter into a greased and floured 8½ inch (22 cm) springform pan.

◆ Bake 45 to 50 minutes or until toothpick inserted in centre comes out clean. Cool.

◆ Decorate with icing and chocolate-dipped nuts.

Prep time: 30 minutes
Baking time: 50 minutes
Makes 10 to 12 servings.

BUNNY CUT-UP CAKE

Cake

1½ cups	all-purpose flour	375 mL
1⅓ cups	sugar	325 mL
1 tsp	baking soda	5 mL
¾ tsp	salt	3 mL
½ cup	butter or margarine, softened	125 mL
1 cup	milk	250 mL
1 tsp	vanilla	5 mL
2	eggs	2
3	squares BAKER'S Unsweetened Chocolate, melted and cooled	3

Icing

2	egg whites	2
1½ cups	sugar	375 mL
	Dash of salt	
½ cup	water	125 mL
1 Tbsp	corn syrup	15 mL
1 tsp	vanilla	5 mL

Chocolate Coconut

3 cups	BAKER'S ANGEL FLAKE Coconut	750 mL
2	squares BAKER'S Semi-Sweet Chocolate, melted and cooled	2

Pink Coconut

¼ cup	BAKER'S ANGEL FLAKE Coconut	50 mL
	One drop red food colouring	

White Coconut

1 cup	BAKER'S ANGEL FLAKE Coconut	250 mL
	Assorted candies	

Cake:

◆ Heat oven to 350°F (180°C).

◆ Combine flour with sugar, baking soda and salt.

◆ Cream butter. Add flour mixture, milk and vanilla. Beat at medium speed of electric mixer for 2 minutes.

◆ Add eggs and chocolate. Beat one minute more.

◆ Pour batter into two greased and floured 9 inch (23 cm) cake pans. Bake for 30 to 35 minutes or until toothpick inserted in centre comes out clean. Cool in pans 10 minutes. Remove and finish cooling on racks.

◆ Cut cake according to photo. Arrange on large tray or cookie sheet.

Icing:

◆ Combine egg whites, sugar, salt, water and corn syrup in top of double boiler or in heat-proof bowl.

◆ Beat on low speed of electric mixer for 1 minute. Place over boiling water and beat constantly at high speed for 7 minutes or until stiff peaks form. Remove from water.

◆ Add vanilla and beat for 1 minute more or until thick enough to spread.

Chocolate Coconut:

◆ Combine coconut and melted chocolate; rub with hands to distribute chocolate evenly.

Pink Coconut:

◆ Combine coconut and food colouring; rub with hands to distribute colour evenly.

To Assemble Cake:

◆ Place a small amount of icing between cake pieces to hold them in place. Ice top and sides to give appearance of a single piece of cake, rounding off corners.

◆ Sprinkle with chocolate coconut for body, pink coconut for inside of ears and white coconut for bow tie. Decorate with assorted candies to make eyes, bow tie and whiskers.

Prep time: 1 hour
Baking time: 35 minutes
Makes 12 servings.

Cut one round cake to make ears and bow tie.

Arrange cake pieces to make a bunny.

Ice entire cake joining all pieces.

Sprinkle with coconut.

Decorate with candies.

TEDDY BEAR CUT-UP CAKE

Cake

	Refer to cake recipe in Bunny Cut-Up Cake (p. 102)	
6	KRAFT Marshmallows	6

Icing

2	egg whites	2
1½ cups	sugar	375 mL
	Dash of salt	
½ cup	water	125 mL
1 Tbsp	corn syrup	15 mL
1¼ tsp	vanilla	6 mL

Chocolate Coconut

2¼ cups	BAKER'S ANGEL FLAKE Coconut	550 mL
2	squares BAKER'S Semi-Sweet Chocolate, melted and cooled	2

Decorations

½ cup	BAKER'S ANGEL FLAKE Coconut	125 mL
	Assorted candies	
2	Chocolate wafers	2

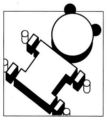

Cake:

◆ Distribute batter between an 8 inch (20 cm) round cake pan and a 9 inch (23 cm) square pan. Bake.

◆ Cut cake according to diagram. Arrange on large tray. Add 4 marshmallows to make paws.

Icing:

◆ Combine egg whites, sugar, salt, water and corn syrup in top of a double boiler or in heat-proof bowl.

◆ Beat on low speed of electric mixer for 1 minute. Place over boiling water and beat constantly at high speed for 7 minutes or until stiff peaks form. Remove from water.

◆ Add vanilla and beat for 1 minute more or until thick enough to spread.

Chocolate Coconut:

◆ Combine coconut and melted chocolate; rub with hands to distribute chocolate evenly.

To Assemble Cake:

◆ Place a small amount of icing between cake pieces to hold them in place. Ice top and sides to give appearance of a single piece of cake, rounding off corners.

◆ Sprinkle white coconut over face, tummy and paws; chocolate coconut over the rest.

◆ Decorate with assorted candies to make face and buttons; chocolate wafers supported by a marshmallow for each ear.

Prep time: 1 hour
Baking time: 35 minutes
Makes 12 servings.

EASY EASTER EGGS

Make your own Easter cream eggs.

1 pkg (4 serving size)	JELL-O Instant Pudding, any flavour	1 pkg (4 serving size)	
⅓ cup	boiling water	75 mL	
⅓ cup	butter or margarine	75 mL	
3 cups	icing sugar, sifted	750 mL	
6	squares *each* BAKER'S White and Semi-Sweet Chocolate	6	
	Coloured sprinkles		

◆ Stir pudding, water and butter in a large bowl until smooth.

◆ Mix in icing sugar by cupfuls, stirring until mixture forms a ball. Form into 1½ inch (3 cm) egg shapes. Refrigerate.

◆ Partially melt *each* chocolate over hot water. Remove from heat and continue stirring until melted and smooth. Dip eggs into chocolate. Decorate with leftover melted chocolate and coloured sprinkles.

Prep time: 30 minutes plus chilling
Makes 2 dozen eggs.

BITTERSWEET CHOCOLATE FONDUE

A delicious dessert idea that friends and family will love –
and it's so simple to prepare.

6	squares BAKER'S Bittersweet Chocolate	6
⅓ cup	light cream (18% b.f.)	75 mL
3 Tbsp	liqueur, brandy or rum (optional)	45 mL
	Assorted fresh fruit pieces or cake cubes	

◆ Melt chocolate with cream over low heat or in microwave on MEDIUM power 2 to 3 minutes; blend until smooth.

◆ Stir in liqueur. If liqueur is not desired, substitute with an additional 3 Tbsp (45 mL) cream.

◆ Transfer to serving dish or fondue pot. Serve warm with fresh fruit.

◆ For White Chocolate Fondue, use 6 squares Baker's White Chocolate, 3 Tbsp (45 mL) whipping cream (35% b.f.) and 2 Tbsp (30 mL) orange liqueur. Proceed as above.

Prep time: 15 minutes
Makes 4 servings.

HEAVENLY CHOCOLATE ICE CREAM PIE

Make your own ice cream shop creation.

Crust

1½ cups	chocolate wafer crumbs	375 mL
⅓ cup	butter or margarine, melted	75 mL
4-6 cups	vanilla ice cream, softened	1-1.5 L

Filling

½ cup	butter or margarine, softened	125 mL
¼ cup	sugar	50 mL
4	squares BAKER'S Semi-Sweet Chocolate, melted and cooled	4
1½ tsp	vanilla	7 mL
2	eggs	2
	Chocolate curls or shavings (optional)	

Crust:

◆ Combine crumbs and melted butter; mix well. Press into 9 inch (23 cm) pie plate. Spoon ice cream into bottom and up sides of crust, leaving a depression in centre.

◆ Freeze until firm.

Filling:

◆ Cream butter. Gradually add sugar, creaming well after each addition. Beat 3 minutes at medium speed of electric mixer. Add chocolate and vanilla; blend well.

◆ Add eggs, one at a time, beating for 2 minutes at medium speed after each addition. Spoon into centre of ice cream shell; freeze until firm, about 3 hours.

◆ Garnish with chocolate curls or shavings, if desired.

◆ To serve, remove from freezer and dip pie plate in hot water for about one minute to release crust. Let stand 15 minutes at room temperature before serving. Store any leftover pie covered, in freezer.

Prep time: 20 minutes plus freezing
Makes 8 servings.

FRENCH CHOCOLATE PIE

½ cup	butter or margarine	125 mL
¾ cup	sugar	175 mL
2	squares BAKER'S Unsweetened Chocolate, melted and cooled	2
2	eggs	2
1 cont. (500 mL)	COOL WHIP Whipped Topping, thawed	1 cont. (500 mL)
1	baked 9 inch (23 cm) pie shell, cooled	1
	Chocolate leaves (optional)	

◆ Cream butter and sugar. Stir in chocolate.

◆ Add eggs, one at a time, beating at high speed for 5 minutes after each addition.

◆ Fold chocolate mixture into whipped topping; blend well. Pour into pie shell.

◆ Chill at least 2 hours. Garnish with chocolate leaves, if desired.

Prep time: 15 minutes plus chilling
Makes 8 servings.

1

Drizzle lined bowl with melted chocolate.

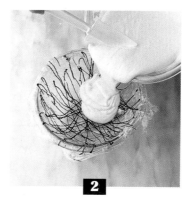

2

Pour white mousse into bowl. Freeze.

3

Pour dark mousse over white mousse. Freeze.

DOUBLE CHOCOLATE BOMBE

A wonderful frozen white and dark chocolate bombe.
Easy to make ahead!

White Mousse

1	square BAKER'S Semi-Sweet Chocolate, melted	1
1 env. (7 g)	unflavoured gelatin	1 env. (7 g)
⅔ cup	whipping cream	150 mL
6	squares BAKER'S White Chocolate, chopped	6
2 Tbsp	butter or margarine	30 mL
2	eggs, separated	2
¼ cup	sugar	50 mL

Dark Mousse

⅓ cup	whipping cream	75 mL
5	squares BAKER'S Semi-Sweet Chocolate, chopped	5
2 Tbsp	butter or margarine	30 mL
2	eggs, separated	2
¼ cup	sugar	50 mL

◆ Line a 6 cup (1.5 L) mixing bowl with plastic wrap and drizzle inner surface with melted chocolate; freeze.

White Mousse:

◆ Sprinkle gelatin over cream in saucepan. Let stand 5 minutes. Bring cream to a boil; remove from heat. Add white chocolate and butter; stir until melted. Blend into egg yolks.

◆ Beat egg whites until frothy; gradually add sugar, beating until stiff peaks form. Fold into chocolate mixture; pour into prepared bowl. Freeze 30 minutes.

Dark Mousse:

◆ Prepare dark mousse layer following white mousse directions, omitting gelatin step.

◆ Pour over white chocolate mixture. Smooth surface with a knife or spatula.

◆ Freeze until set, at least 8 hours. Unmould onto serving plate, remove plastic wrap.

Prep time: 30 minutes plus freezing
Makes 8 to 10 servings.

4

Unmould onto serving plate.

5

Remove plastic wrap.

FROZEN TIRAMISU CAKE

1 (298 g)	frozen pound cake, partially defrosted, sliced	1 (298 g)
3 Tbsp	dark rum	45 mL
2 Tbsp	coffee liqueur	30 mL
2	eggs, at room temperature	2
½ cup	sugar	125 mL
½ tsp	vanilla	2 mL
2 pkgs (250 g each)	PHILADELPHIA BRAND Cream Cheese, softened	2 pkgs (250 g each)
1	egg white, at room temperature	1
3	squares BAKER'S Semi-Sweet Chocolate, grated	3
1 cont. (500 mL)	coffee ice cream, softened	1 cont. (500 mL)

◆ Place pound cake slices on cookie sheet and toast in oven at 350°F (180°C) for 10 minutes, or until golden and dry. Combine rum and liqueur and brush both sides of slices; cool on rack.

◆ Line two loaf pans, 9 × 5 inch (23 × 13 cm) with plastic wrap.

◆ Beat eggs and sugar with electric mixer until mixture is thick and very pale. Beat in vanilla and cream cheese, combining well.

◆ Beat egg white until it holds soft peaks and fold it into cheese mixture. Pour mixture into 1 of the prepared loaf pans. Freeze until firm, about 3 hours.

◆ To assemble, arrange 1 row of cake slices, overlapping slightly, in bottom of *other* loaf pan. Pack in half of the frozen cheese mixture, smoothing top. Sprinkle with half of grated chocolate.

◆ Arrange another layer of cake slices, overlapping slightly to cover chocolate completely. Pack in ice cream, smoothing top. Sprinkle with remaining grated chocolate. Repeat without ice cream.

◆ Arrange another layer of cake slices in the same manner; top with remaining cheese mixture. Arrange any remaining cake slices on top, packing cake in firmly. Cover with plastic wrap over top and freeze cake overnight.

◆ Invert cake onto serving dish, discarding plastic wrap. Serve sliced with your favourite chocolate sauce laced with rum or coffee liqueur, if desired.

Prep time: 45 minutes
Freezing time: 3 hours plus overnight
Makes 8 servings.

FABULOUS FUDGE RIBBON CAKE

Cheese Mixture

1 pkg (250 g)	PHILADELPHIA BRAND Cream Cheese, softened	1 pkg (250 g)	
¼ cup	sugar	50 mL	
1	egg	1	
½ tsp	vanilla	2 mL	

Cake

1 cup	all-purpose flour	250 mL	
1⅓ cups	sugar	325 mL	
1¼ tsp	baking powder	6 mL	
½ tsp	salt	2 mL	
¼ tsp	baking soda	1 mL	
1 cup	milk	250 mL	
3 Tbsp	butter or margarine	45 mL	
1	egg	1	
½ tsp	vanilla	2 mL	
3	squares BAKER'S Unsweetened Chocolate, melted and cooled	3	

Chocolate Glaze

3	squares BAKER'S Semi-Sweet Chocolate	3	
1 Tbsp	butter or margarine	15 mL	
1 Tbsp	water	15 mL	
½ tsp	vegetable oil	2 mL	

Cheese Mixture:

◆ Beat cheese, sugar, egg and vanilla until smooth. Set aside.

Cake:

◆ Heat oven to 350°F (180°C).

◆ Combine cake ingredients. Blend 30 seconds on low speed of electric mixer. Beat 2 minutes on medium speed.

◆ Pour half of batter into greased 9 inch (23 cm) square pan. Cover evenly with cheese mixture. Top with remaining cake batter to cover completely.

◆ Bake for 50 to 55 minutes or until toothpick inserted in centre comes out clean. Cool.

Chocolate Glaze:

◆ Melt chocolate with butter, water, and oil over low heat; blend until smooth. Spread evenly over cake.

Prep time: 40 minutes
Baking time: 55 minutes
Makes 9 servings.

BITTERSWEET CHOCOLATE MOUSSE FLAN

A delicious chocolate flan with a sea of luscious mousse.

Pastry

1 cup	all-purpose flour	250 mL
2 Tbsp	icing sugar	30 mL
2	squares BAKER'S Bittersweet Chocolate, melted	2
½ cup	butter, softened	125 mL

Mousse Filling

⅓ cup	whipping cream	75 mL
5	squares BAKER'S Bittersweet Chocolate, chopped	5
2 Tbsp	butter	30 mL
2	eggs, separated	2
¼ cup	sugar	50 mL

Garnish

3	squares BAKER'S Bittersweet Chocolate, coarsely grated	3
	Icing sugar	

Pastry:

◆ Combine flour, sugar and chocolate. Cut in butter until mixture resembles coarse crumbs; form into ball. (Can use food processor.)

◆ Press into bottom and up sides of 9½ inch (24 cm) flan pan with removable bottom. Chill for 1 hour.

◆ Heat oven to 425°F (220°C). Bake for 10 minutes; cool.

Mousse Filling:

◆ Bring cream to a boil. Add chocolate and butter; stir until melted. Blend in egg yolks; remove from heat.

◆ Beat egg whites until frothy; gradually add sugar beating until stiff peaks form. Fold into chocolate mixture; pour into pastry crust. Chill 5 minutes.

Garnish:

◆ Sprinkle chocolate over mousse. Chill for 3 hours.

◆ Before serving lay 1 inch (2.5 cm) strips of wax paper over flan leaving 1 inch (2.5 cm) spaces in between. Dust generously with icing sugar. Remove strips of wax paper.

Prep time: 40 minutes plus chilling
Baking time: 10 minutes
Makes 12 servings.

1

Dip balloon into chocolate.

2

Spread chocolate evenly over surface.

3

Place on cookie sheet and freeze until firm.

BITTERSWEET CHOCOLATE MOUSSE

6	squares BAKER'S Bittersweet Chocolate, melted and cooled	6
3	eggs	3
2 Tbsp	coffee liqueur	30 mL
3 Tbsp	icing sugar, sifted	45 mL
1 cup	whipping cream, whipped	250 mL

◆ Combine chocolate, 1 whole egg and 2 egg yolks; mix well. Blend in liqueur.

◆ Beat 2 egg whites until foamy. Add icing sugar and beat until stiff shiny peaks form.

◆ Fold whipping cream into egg whites. Carefully fold chocolate mixture into egg white mixture.

◆ Pour into Chocolate Balloon Cups or individual dishes. Chill 3 hours.

Prep time: 20 minutes plus chilling
Makes 4 to 6 servings.

CHOCOLATE BALLOON CUPS

This is an easy way to impress your guests!

6	squares BAKER'S Bittersweet Chocolate, partially melted	6
4	small balloons	4

◆ Blow balloons to desired size for cups.

◆ Dip round end of each balloon into chocolate. Spread evenly over surface to make the shape of a cup.

◆ Stand chocolate end on wax paper-lined cookie sheet.

◆ Freeze 20 minutes.

◆ Let stand at room temperature 5 minutes. Pop balloon; remove carefully.

◆ Fill with mousse.

Prep time: 15 minutes plus freezing
Makes 4 dessert cups.

Pop balloons and remove.

Fill with mousse.

ORANGE WHITE CHOCOLATE MOUSSE CAKE

An elegant finish to a special dinner.

Crust

¾ cup	graham crumbs	175 mL
2 Tbsp	sugar	30 mL
¼ cup	butter or margarine, melted	50 mL
1 tsp	grated orange rind	5 mL

Mousse

1 env. (7 g)	unflavoured gelatin	1 env. (7g)
1 cup	orange juice	250 mL
6	squares BAKER'S White Chocolate, melted and cooled	6
1 cup	whipping cream, whipped	250 mL
3	egg whites	3

Candied orange peel (optional)

3	oranges	3
1 cup	sugar	250 mL
1½ cups	water, divided	375 mL

Crust:

◆ Grease and wax paper line sides of an 8½ inch (22 cm) springform pan.

◆ Combine crumbs, sugar, butter and orange rind and press onto bottom of prepared pan; chill.

Mousse:

◆ Sprinkle gelatin over orange juice in saucepan. Let stand 5 minutes to soften. Stir mixture over low heat until gelatin is dissolved; cool.

◆ Fold chocolate into whipped cream. Gradually stir in gelatin mixture until well blended.

◆ Beat egg whites until stiff peaks form; fold into chocolate mixture. Pour mixture over crust. Chill for 3 hours or until set.

◆ Garnish with candied orange peel, if desired.

Prep time: 30 minutes plus chilling time Makes 16 servings.

Candied Orange Peel:

◆ Cut rind from oranges into thin strips leaving no white showing. Boil rind in 1 cup (250 mL) water for 3 minutes.

◆ Strain and discard water. Bring sugar and remaining water to a boil.

◆ Add rind and boil for 5 minutes; strain. Cool on rack.

CHOCOLATE CARROT CAKE

A recipe for the times – chocolate and carrot cake.

Cake

4	eggs	4
2 cups	sugar	500 mL
1 cup	vegetable oil	250 mL
4	squares BAKER'S Unsweetened Chocolate, melted	4
2 cups	all-purpose flour	500 mL
2 tsp	baking powder	10 mL
1 tsp	baking soda	5 mL
1 Tbsp	cinnamon	15 mL
	Pinch of cloves and nutmeg	
½ tsp	salt	2 mL
2 cups	grated carrots	500 mL
1 can (19 oz)	crushed pineapple, well drained	1 can (540 mL)
1 tsp	vanilla	5 mL
½ cup	chopped walnuts or pecans	125 mL

Icing

6	squares BAKER'S Semi-Sweet Chocolate, chopped	6
3 Tbsp	water	45 mL
1 pkg (250 g)	PHILADELPHIA BRAND Cream Cheese, softened	1 pkg (250 g)
1 tsp	vanilla	5 mL
1½ cups	icing sugar, sifted	375 mL

Cake:

- ◆ Heat oven to 350°F (180°C).
- ◆ Beat eggs until frothy. Gradually add sugar, oil and melted chocolate, beating until light.
- ◆ Combine dry ingredients. Add to egg mixture; mix well.
- ◆ Fold in remaining ingredients. Pour into greased and floured 10 inch (25 cm) bundt or tube pan.
- ◆ Bake for 50 minutes or until toothpick inserted in centre comes out clean. Invert on rack and cool.

Icing:

- ◆ Melt chocolate with water over low heat or in microwave on HIGH 2 minutes. Stir until chocolate is completely melted and smooth.
- ◆ Beat cream cheese and vanilla. Beat in melted chocolate. Gradually beat in icing sugar until smooth. Spread on top of cake.

Prep time: 20 minutes
Baking time: 50 minutes
Makes 12 servings.

BLACK FOREST TORTE

A chocolate-cherry European tradition.

Cake

4	squares BAKER'S Sweet Chocolate	4
⅓ cup	water	75 mL
¾ cup	butter or margarine, softened	175 mL
1⅓ cups	sugar	325 mL
3	eggs, separated	3
¾ tsp	vanilla	3 mL
1¾ cups	all-purpose flour	425 mL
¼ tsp	salt	1 mL
¾ tsp	baking soda	3 mL
¾ cup	buttermilk or soured milk*	175 mL

Icing

⅓ cup	cherry liqueur (optional)	75 mL
1 can (14 oz)	pitted sour cherries	1 can (398 mL)
2 Tbsp	cornstarch	30 mL
3 cups	whipping cream	750 mL
3 Tbsp	sugar	45 mL
2 tsp	vanilla	10 mL
4	squares BAKER'S Sweet Chocolate, grated	4
	Maraschino cherries	

* To sour milk, place 2 tsp (10 mL) vinegar in a measuring cup; fill with milk to 1 cup (175 mL) level.

Cake:

◆ Heat oven to 350°F (180°C).

◆ Melt chocolate with water in small saucepan over low heat or in microwave on MEDIUM power for 2 minutes. Stir until smooth; cool.

◆ Beat butter and sugar until light and fluffy. Add egg yolks, one at a time, beating after each addition. Add vanilla and melted chocolate; blend well.

◆ Combine flour, salt and baking soda.

◆ Alternately blend in flour mixture and sour milk, one-third at a time on low speed of electric mixer.

◆ Beat egg whites until stiff peaks form. Fold into cake batter. Pour into two greased and floured 9 inch (23 cm) cake pans. Bake for 30 minutes or until cake springs back when lightly pressed. Cool.

Filling and Icing:

◆ Cut each cake layer horizontally. Brush cut surfaces with cherry liqueur. Drain cherries reserving syrup. Cut cherries in half. Combine syrup and cornstarch. Bring to a boil over medium heat and boil for 1 minute, stirring constantly. Stir in cherries. Chill.

◆ Beat cream with sugar and vanilla until stiff peaks form.

◆ Spread bottom layer with half the cherry filling. Spread second layer with 1 cup (250 mL) of the whipped cream. Use remaining cherry filling on third layer; top with the fourth layer. Cover entire cake with remaining whipped cream. Garnish sides of cake with grated chocolate and decorate top with maraschino cherries.

Prep time: 60 minutes
Baking time: 30 minutes
Makes 10 servings.

CHOCOLATE CHERRY DREAM CAKE

Cake

4	squares BAKER'S Unsweetened Chocolate	4
½ cup	butter or margarine	125 mL
2 cups	sugar	500 mL
½ tsp	vanilla	2 mL
¼ tsp	salt	1 mL
2	eggs	2
½ cup	sour cream	125 mL
1½ tsp	baking soda	7 mL
2 cups	all-purpose flour	500 mL
1 cup	boiling water	250 mL
	Icing sugar	
	Whipped cream	

Warm Cherry Sauce

1 can (14 oz)	pitted sweet black cherries	1 can (398 mL)
2 Tbsp	cornstarch	30 mL
2 Tbsp	sugar	30 mL
¼ cup	water	50 mL
¼ cup	burgundy or other red wine	50 mL

Cake:

◆ Heat oven to 350°F (180°C).

◆ Melt chocolate with butter over low heat; cool. Add sugar, vanilla, and salt, mix well.

◆ Add eggs, one at a time, beating well after each addition.

◆ Combine sour cream and baking soda; mix well. Alternately blend in sour cream and flour one-third at a time on low speed of electric mixer. Add boiling water; blend well. Batter will be thin. Pour into greased and floured 10 inch (25 cm) bundt or tube pan.

◆ Bake for 45 to 50 minutes or until toothpick inserted in centre comes out clean. Cool on wire rack.

◆ Dust with icing sugar. Fill centre of cake with whipped cream.

Warm Cherry Sauce:

◆ Drain cherries, reserving syrup.

◆ Combine cornstarch and sugar in saucepan. Gradually add reserved syrup and water.

◆ Cook and stir over medium heat until mixture comes to a full bubbling boil and boil 1 minute. Stir in cherries and wine.

◆ Top each slice with a dollop of whipped cream and a generous spoonful of cherry sauce. Store leftover cake in refrigerator.

Prep time: 1 hour
Baking time: 50 minutes
Makes 12 servings.

GRASSHOPPER PIE

Chocolate Crust

6	squares BAKER'S Semi-Sweet Chocolate, chopped	6
2 Tbsp	butter or margarine	30 mL

Filling

2	envelopes DREAM WHIP Dessert Topping Mix, prepared	2
1 pkg (85 g)	JELL-O Lime Jelly Powder	1 pkg (85 g)
⅔ cup	boiling water	150 mL
2 cups	ice cubes	500 mL
2 Tbsp	mint liqueur	30 mL
1 Tbsp	white cocoa liqueur	15 mL
	Mint leaves (optional)	

Chocolate Crust:

◆ Partially melt chocolate with butter over low heat.

◆ Line a 9 inch (23 cm) pie plate with plastic wrap, covering bottom and sides evenly. Spoon chocolate mixture evenly over plastic wrap, forming a crust. Chill until firm, about 1 hour.

◆ Carefully remove plastic wrap. Place chocolate shell back in pie plate. Chill.

Filling:

◆ Thoroughly dissolve jelly powder in boiling water. Add ice cubes and stir constantly until jelly starts to thicken, about 2 to 3 minutes. Remove any unmelted ice. Add liqueurs to jelly.

◆ Stir in prepared dessert topping and beat with an electric mixer until well blended. Spoon into crust. Garnish with chocolate or mint leaves, if desired. Chill 3 hours.

Prep time: 30 minutes plus chilling
Makes 8 servings.

WHITE CHOCOLATE CRÈME BRÛLÉE

Serve this with fresh raspberries for the perfect dessert.

5	egg yolks	5
½ cup	sugar, divided	125 mL
2 cups	whipping cream	500 mL
3	squares BAKER'S White Chocolate, chopped	3
¼ tsp	vanilla	1 mL
3	squares BAKER'S White Chocolate, melted	3

◆ Heat oven to 300°F (150°C).

◆ Whisk egg yolks and ¼ cup (50 mL) sugar in medium bowl.

◆ Bring cream and remaining sugar to simmer in heavy medium saucepan. Reduce heat to low. Gradually add chopped chocolate to cream mixture and whisk until smooth.

◆ Gradually whisk hot chocolate mixture into yolk mixture. Mix in vanilla.

◆ Ladle custard into six 6 oz (175 mL) custard cups. Place cups in large baking pan. Add enough hot water to pan to come halfway up sides of cups. Bake until custards are set in centre, about 50 minutes. Remove custards from water and cool. Cover and refrigerate overnight.

◆ Drizzle top of each custard with melted chocolate.

Prep time: 10 minutes
Baking time: 50 minutes
Makes 6 servings.

CHOCOLATE PECAN PIE

3	eggs	3
1 cup	sugar	250 mL
½ tsp	salt	2 mL
⅓ cup	melted butter	75 mL
1 cup	corn syrup	250 mL
2	squares BAKER'S Unsweetened Chocolate, melted and cooled	2
1 cup	pecan halves	250 mL
1 tsp	vanilla	5 mL
1	unbaked 9 inch (23 cm) pie shell	1
	Whipped cream (optional)	

◆ Heat oven to 375°F (190°C).

◆ Combine eggs, sugar, salt, butter, and corn syrup; mix well. Blend in chocolate, pecans and vanilla. Pour into pie shell.

◆ Bake for 50 to 60 minutes. The top should still be soft and the centre not quite set when the pie is shaken. Cool on rack. Serve with whipped cream, if desired.

Prep time: 15 minutes
Baking time: 1 hour
Makes 8 servings.

TIRAMISU

BAKER'S KITCHENS version of an Italian classic.

4	egg yolks	4
1 cup	sugar	250 mL
1 tsp	vanilla	5 mL
2 pkgs (250 g each)	PHILADELPHIA BRAND Cream Cheese, softened	2 pkgs (250 g each)
¼ cup	strongly brewed coffee	50 mL
¼ cup	dark rum	50 mL
2 pkgs (3 oz each)	ladyfingers (soft type) cut in half, lengthwise	2 pkgs (85 g each)
1 cup	whipping cream, whipped	250 mL
8	squares BAKER'S Semi-Sweet Chocolate, coarsely grated	8
	Strawberries (optional)	

◆ Combine egg yolks, sugar and vanilla in food processor with metal blade or mixing bowl. Process or beat until pale yellow, about 2 minutes. Gradually add cheese and blend until smooth. Chill 1 hour.

◆ Meanwhile, combine coffee and rum; brush over ladyfingers.

◆ Fold whipped cream into cheese mixture. Line bottom of narrow, straight sided, glass trifle bowl with ¼ of the ladyfingers. Spread ¼ of cheese mixture over ladyfingers; sprinkle with ¼ of the grated chocolate. Repeat making 3 more layers. Cover tightly; chill 4 hours or overnight to blend flavours. Garnish with grated chocolate and strawberries, if desired.

Prep time: 30 minutes plus chilling
Serves 10 to 12.

Chocolate Pecan Pie

TRIPLE CHOCOLATE TREASURE CAKE

This is real death by chocolate!

Cake

1¾ cups	sugar	425 mL
1¾ cups	all-purpose flour	425 mL
2 tsp	baking soda	10 mL
1 tsp	baking powder	5 mL
½ tsp	salt	2 mL
5	squares BAKER'S Unsweetened Chocolate, melted	5
1 cup	strong black coffee, lukewarm	250 mL
¾ cup	sour cream	175 mL
¼ cup	vegetable oil	50 mL
1 tsp	vanilla	5 mL

Filling

6	squares BAKER'S White Chocolate, chopped	6
¼ cup	butter	50 mL
¼ cup	whipping cream	50 mL

Garnish

	Whipped cream	
2	squares BAKER'S Bittersweet Chocolate, melted	2

Cake:

◆ Heat oven to 350°F (180°C).

◆ Combine all ingredients for cake in a large mixing bowl and beat on high speed of electric mixer for 2 minutes.

◆ Pour into greased and floured 9 inch (23 cm) springform pan.

◆ Bake for 45 to 50 minutes or until toothpick inserted in centre comes out clean. This cake will have a slight dip in the centre.

◆ Cool 10 minutes; remove sides of pan. Push the handle end of wooden spoon into cake to make deep holes over entire surface of cake.

Filling:

◆ Melt white chocolate and butter with whipping cream over very low heat. Stir until smooth; cool slightly.

◆ Pour filling into holes in cake; chill.

◆ Just before serving, garnish top with whipped cream and melted chocolate. Decorate as desired.

Prep time: 20 minutes
Baking time: 50 minutes
Makes 12 servings.

Beat together all cake ingredients.

Pour batter into prepared pan.

Push the handle of wooden spoon into cake to make deep holes.

4

Prepare filling.

5

Pour filling into holes.

6

Garnish cake with whipped cream and drizzle with chocolate.

TRIPLE CHOCOLATE RASPBERRY FANTASY

Decadent layers of brownie, cheesecake,
raspberry and chocolate!

Brownie Layer

3	squares BAKER'S Unsweetened Chocolate	3
2	squares BAKER'S Bittersweet Chocolate	2
½ cup	butter or margarine	125 mL
2	eggs	2
1¼ cups	packed brown sugar	300 mL
¾ cup	all-purpose flour	175 mL
¼ tsp	baking powder	1 mL

White Chocolate Layer

1 pkg (250 g)	PHILADELPHIA BRAND Cream Cheese, softened	1 pkg (250 g)
⅔ cup	icing sugar, sifted	150 mL
2 Tbsp	raspberry liqueur (optional)	30 mL
3	squares BAKER'S White Chocolate, melted and cooled	3
1	egg	1

Topping

½ cup	raspberry jam	125 mL
½ cup	whipping cream	125 mL
4	squares BAKER'S Bittersweet Chocolate, chopped	4
	White chocolate curls and raspberries	

Brownie Layer:

◆ Melt chocolates and butter over low heat.

◆ Beat eggs and sugar on high speed of electric mixer for 5 minutes, or until thick and lemon-coloured. Fold in chocolate mixture, flour and baking powder.

◆ Pour into greased and floured 10 inch (25 cm) pie plate or springform pan.

White Chocolate Layer:

◆ Heat oven to 325°F (160°C).

◆ Beat cream cheese, icing sugar, liqueur, chocolate and egg in medium bowl with electric mixer until blended and smooth.

◆ Randomly spoon white mixture onto brownie layer, leaving a space between each spoonful.

◆ Bake for 45 to 55 minutes until toothpick inserted in centre comes out almost clean. Cool.

Topping:

◆ Spoon jam evenly over entire surface of pie.

◆ Heat cream with chocolate over low heat or in microwave on MEDIUM power for 3 to 4 minutes; stir until melted and smooth.

◆ Pour over top of pie, spreading evenly. Chill to set glaze. Garnish with white chocolate curls and raspberries.

Prep time: 40 minutes plus chilling
Baking time: 55 minutes
Makes about 12 servings.

CHOCOLATE STRAWBERRY SHORTCAKE

Chocolate and strawberries – a great combination!

Cake

1½ cups	all-purpose flour	375 mL
½ tsp	baking soda	2 mL
½ tsp	salt	2 mL
1 Tbsp	baking powder	15 mL
½ cup	sugar	125 mL
⅓ cup	butter or margarine	75 mL
1 cup	soured milk*	250 mL
2	squares BAKER'S Unsweetened Chocolate, melted and cooled	2
2 Tbsp	sugar	30 mL
1 Tbsp	packed brown sugar	15 mL
2 Tbsp	orange liqueur or orange juice	30 mL

Topping

3	squares BAKER'S Semi-Sweet Chocolate	3
1 Tbsp	butter or margarine	15 mL
1 qt	strawberries	1 L
1 cont. (1 L)	COOL WHIP Whipped Topping, thawed	1 cont. (1 L)

* Place 1 Tbsp (15 mL) vinegar in a measuring cup and add milk to 1 cup (250 mL) mark.

Cake:

◆ Heat oven to 400°F (200°C).

◆ Combine flour, baking soda, salt, baking powder and ½ cup (125 mL) sugar. Cut in butter until mixture resembles coarse meal. Blend in milk and chocolate; mix well.

◆ Spread into 2 greased and floured 9 inch (23 cm) cake pans.

◆ Combine 2 Tbsp (30 mL) sugar and brown sugar; sprinkle over both layers. Bake for about 10 to 12 minutes or until cake begins to pull away from sides of pan. Cool.

◆ Brush each cake layer with 1 Tbsp (15 mL) of liqueur.

Topping:

◆ Melt chocolate with butter over low heat.

◆ Wash strawberries and dry thoroughly. For garnish on top of cake, dip bottom of ten whole strawberries in chocolate. Place on waxed paper. Chill until chocolate is firm. Hull and slice remaining berries.

To Assemble Cake:

◆ Place one cake layer on serving plate and top with all the sliced strawberries and half of whipped topping.

◆ Cover with second cake layer. Top with remaining whipped topping and whole dipped strawberries. Drizzle remaining melted chocolate over top of cake. Refrigerate.

Prep time: 40 minutes
Baking time: 12 minutes
Makes 12 servings.

WHITE CHOCOLATE MOUSSE

6	squares BAKER'S White Chocolate, chopped	6	
2 cups	whipping cream	500 mL	
1 tsp	vanilla	5 mL	
	Fresh raspberries		

◆ Melt white chocolate with cream over low heat until smooth, stirring constantly. Add vanilla.

◆ Pour into bowl and cover. Refrigerate overnight or until very cold and thickened.

◆ Beat mixture on high with mixer until fluffy and light. DO NOT OVERBEAT or mixture will curdle.

◆ Pour into dessert cups. Garnish with raspberries.

Prep time: 20 minutes
Makes 6 servings.

CHEESECAKES

DECADENT CHOCOLATE CHIP CHEESECAKE

Crust

1 cup	chocolate wafer crumbs	250 mL
2 Tbsp	melted butter or margarine	30 mL

Filling

3 pkgs (250 g each)	PHILADELPHIA BRAND Cream Cheese, softened	3 pkgs (250 g each)
1 cup	sugar	250 mL
3	eggs at room temperature	3
½ cup	sour cream	125 mL
1 Tbsp	vanilla	15 mL
1 pkg (300 g)	BAKER'S Semi-Sweet Chocolate Chips	1 pkg (300 g)
or 1 pkg (225 g)	BAKER'S White Chocolate Chips	1 pkg (225 g)

Glaze

½ cup	whipping cream	125 mL
4	squares BAKER'S Semi-Sweet Chocolate, chopped	4

Crust:

◆ Mix wafer crumbs and butter. Press firmly onto bottom of 9 inch (23 cm) springform pan.

Filling:

◆ Heat oven to 350°F (180°C).

◆ Beat cream cheese and sugar with an electric mixer until smooth. Beat in eggs one at a time, until just blended. Beat in sour cream and vanilla. Stir in chocolate chips. Pour into pan.

◆ Bake for 50 minutes or until centre of cake is just set. Remove from oven and run sharp knife around edge of cake to loosen cake and prevent cracking. Cool completely on rack; chill overnight. Remove pan rim.

Glaze:

◆ Bring cream to simmer over low heat. Add chocolate and stir until melted and smooth. Pour glaze over top of cake. Garnish as desired.

Prep time: 15 minutes plus chilling
Baking time: 50 minutes
Makes 16 servings.

WHITE CHOCOLATE CHEESECAKE

Filling

2 pkgs (250 g each)	PHILADELPHIA BRAND Cream Cheese, softened	2 pkgs (250 g each)
⅓ cup	sugar	75 mL
1 tsp	lemon juice	5 mL
6	squares BAKER'S White Chocolate, melted and cooled	6
¾ cup	sour cream	175 mL
2	eggs, at room temperature	2
1 tsp	vanilla	5 mL

Topping

1 cup	sour cream	250 mL
2 Tbsp	sugar	30 mL
	White chocolate curls	

Filling:

◆ Heat oven to 450°F (230°C).

◆ Beat cream cheese, sugar and lemon juice with electric mixer until smooth. Beat in chocolate, sour cream, eggs and vanilla.

◆ Pour batter into lightly greased 8½ inch (22 cm) springform pan; smooth top.

◆ Bake for 10 minutes. Reduce heat to 250°F (120°C) and bake 30 to 35 minutes longer.

Topping:

◆ Combine sour cream and sugar. Spread over cheesecake; bake 5 minutes longer.

◆ Remove from oven and run knife around rim of pan to loosen cake and prevent cracking. Cool thoroughly at room temperature. Chill.

◆ Garnish with chocolate curls.

Prep time: 15 minutes plus chilling
Baking time: 50 minutes
Makes 10 to 12 servings.

BITTERSWEET CHOCOLATE TRUFFLE CHEESECAKE

Crust

1⅓ cups	chocolate wafer crumbs	325 mL
⅓ cup	butter or margarine, melted	75 mL

Filling

2 pkgs (250 g each)	PHILADELPHIA BRAND Cream Cheese, softened	2 pkgs (250 g each)
1 cup	sugar	250 mL
3	eggs at room temperature	3
¼ cup	cold coffee or coffee liqueur	50 mL
8	squares BAKER'S Bittersweet Chocolate, melted	8
½ cup	sour cream	125 mL

Glaze

½ cup	whipping cream	125 mL
4	squares BAKER'S Bittersweet Chocolate	4

Crust:

◆ Combine wafer crumbs and butter; press mixture evenly on bottom of 9 inch (23 cm) springform pan.

Filling:

◆ Heat oven to 350°F (180°C).

◆ Beat cream cheese and sugar on lowest speed of electric mixer until smooth. Beat in eggs one at a time. Beat in coffee then chocolate. Blend in sour cream. Pour into prepared pan.

◆ Bake for 40 to 50 minutes or just until centre is barely set. Cool completely on rack, then refrigerate overnight.

Glaze:

◆ Shave a few curls off the back of 4 squares of chocolate. Reserve curls for garnish. Bring cream to a simmer over low heat. Add remaining chocolate and stir until melted and smooth. Spoon over cake. Garnish with curls.

Prep time: 30 minutes plus chilling
Baking time: 50 minutes
Makes about 16 servings.

1

Line springform pan with cookies.

2

Spread chocolate mixture into prepared pan, reserving ½ cup (125 mL).

3

Spread plain mixture over top.

CHOCOLATE AMARETTO CHEESECAKE

Cookie Ring

32	chocolate dipped round wafer cookie rolls	32

Cheesecake

2 pkgs (250 g each)	PHILADELPHIA BRAND Cream Cheese, softened	2 pkgs (250 g each)
¾ cup	packed brown sugar	175 mL
1 env. (7 g)	unflavoured gelatin	1 env. (7 g)
½ cup	almond liqueur	125 mL
1 cup	whipping cream, whipped	250 mL
6	squares BAKER'S Semi-Sweet Chocolate	6

Garnish

1	square BAKER'S Semi-Sweet Chocolate, chopped	1
	Whole unblanched almonds	

Cookie Ring:

◆ Line sides of 8½ inch (22 cm) springform pan with cookies.

Cheesecake:

◆ Beat cream cheese and sugar with electric mixer until smooth.

◆ Sprinkle gelatin over liqueur in saucepan. Let stand 5 minutes to soften. Stir over low heat until gelatin dissolves. Blend warm gelatin into cheese mixture. Fold whipped cream into cheese mixture. Set aside 1 cup (250 mL) of this mixture.

◆ Melt chocolate; cool. Fold into remaining cheese mixture.

◆ Spread all but ½ cup (125 mL) chocolate mixture into prepared pan; spread plain mixture evenly on top. Top with remaining chocolate mixture; swirl with knife to marble. Chill at least 3 hours.

Garnish:

◆ Partially melt chocolate over hot water. Remove from heat and continue stirring until completely melted. Dip almonds into chocolate. Chill. Place on top of cookies.

Prep time: 30 minutes plus chilling
Makes 10 to 12 servings.

4

Spoon remaining chocolate mixture randomly over top of cake.

5

Swirl with knife to marble.

6

Decorate cake with chocolate dipped almonds.

DELUXE CHOCOLATE CHEESECAKE

Cake

2 Tbsp	chocolate wafer crumbs	30 mL
3 pkgs (250 g each)	PHILADELPHIA BRAND Cream Cheese, softened	3 pkgs (250 g each)
1 cup	sugar	250 mL
5	eggs at room temperature	5
1 Tbsp	vanilla	15 mL
6	squares BAKER'S Semi-Sweet Chocolate, melted and cooled	6

Glaze

2	squares BAKER'S Semi-Sweet Chocolate	2
1 Tbsp	butter	15 mL
1 Tbsp	water	15 mL

Rose Leaves

2	squares BAKER'S Semi-Sweet Chocolate, chopped	2
	Rose Leaves	

Cake:

◆ Heat oven to 450°F (230°C).

◆ Grease a 9 inch (23 cm) springform pan. Sprinkle evenly with crumbs.

◆ Beat cream cheese and sugar with electric mixer until smooth. Beat in eggs one at a time. Overbeating will result in cracked surface.

◆ Add vanilla and chocolate; blend well.

◆ Bake for 10 minutes. Reduce oven temperature to 250°F (120°C) and bake 40 minutes longer until centre is almost set.

◆ Remove from oven. Run sharp knife around edge of cake to loosen and prevent cracking. Cool in pan. Chill 8 hours or overnight. Release cake from pan. Remove cake from refrigerator 1 hour before glazing so glaze does not harden immediately.

Glaze:

◆ Melt chocolate, butter and water over low heat.

◆ Spread evenly over cake surface. Garnish with chocolate rose leaves, if desired.

Rose Leaves:

◆ Partially melt chocolate over hot water; remove from heat and continue stirring until completely melted.

◆ With a small brush, spoon or small metal spatula, carefully coat the underside of a fresh leaf that doesn't have any fine hairs on it. The chocolate layer should be about $\frac{1}{16}$ inch (2 mm) thick. Be careful not to get any chocolate on the front side of the leaf. Chill leaf about 15 minutes. Hold leaf by stem to peel off the chocolate. Store in refrigerator.

Prep time: 30 minutes plus chilling
Baking time: 50 minutes
Makes 12 servings.

Orange Chocolate Swirl Cheesecake

Crust

1½ cups	graham crumbs	375 mL
¼ cup	sugar	50 mL
⅓ cup	butter or margarine, melted	75 mL
1 Tbsp	grated orange rind	15 mL

Filling

3 pkgs (250 g each)	PHILADELPHIA BRAND Cream Cheese, softened	3 pkgs (250 g each)
1 cup	sugar	250 mL
5	eggs, at room temperature	5
2 Tbsp	orange liqueur	30 mL
1 tsp	grated orange rind	5 mL
4	squares BAKER'S Semi-Sweet Chocolate, melted and cooled	4

Crust:

◆ Combine crust ingredients. Press onto bottom and 1 inch (2.5 cm) up sides of 9 inch (23 cm) springform pan. Set aside.

Filling:

◆ Heat oven to 350°F (180°C).

◆ Beat cream cheese and sugar with electric mixer until smooth. Beat in eggs one at a time, beating just until blended. Add liqueur and orange rind.

◆ Measure 2 cups (500 mL) of the cheese mixture; fold in chocolate and blend well.

◆ Pour remaining cheese mixture into prepared pan. Add spoonfuls of the chocolate-cheese mixture; draw knife through to marble.

◆ Bake for 35 to 40 minutes. Remove from oven and run knife around rim of pan to loosen cake and prevent cracking. Cool thoroughly at room temperature. Chill.

Prep time: 30 minutes plus chilling
Baking time: 40 minutes
Makes 12 servings.

No-Bake Chocolate Cheesecake

⅓ cup	chopped almonds, toasted	75 mL
2 pkgs (250 g each)	PHILADELPHIA BRAND Cream Cheese, softened	2 pkgs (250 g each)
1 cup	sugar	250 mL
6	squares BAKER'S Semi-Sweet Chocolate, melted and cooled	6
1 env. (7 g)	unflavoured gelatin	1 env. (7 g)
¼ cup	cold water	50 mL
1 cup	whipping cream, whipped	250 mL
2	squares BAKER'S Semi-Sweet Chocolate, chopped	2

◆ Grease 8½ inch (22 cm) springform pan. Sprinkle evenly with almonds.

◆ Beat cream cheese and sugar with electric mixer until smooth. Blend in melted chocolate.

◆ Sprinkle gelatin on top of cold water in saucepan. Let stand 5 minutes to soften. Stir mixture over low heat until gelatin is dissolved. Blend warm gelatin into cheese mixture. Fold cheese mixture into whipped cream. Pour into pan. Chill at least 3 hours.

◆ Partially melt remaining chocolate over hot water. Remove from heat and continue stirring until completely melted. Drizzle on top of cake.

Prep time: 20 minutes plus chilling
Makes 10 to 12 servings.

WHITE CHOCOLATE AND LIME CHEESECAKE

2 pkgs (3 oz each)	soft ladyfingers, halved lengthwise	2 pkgs (85 g each)
2 pkgs (250 g each)	PHILADELPHIA BRAND Cream Cheese, softened	2 pkgs (250 g each)
1 cup	sugar	250 mL
6	squares BAKER'S White Chocolate, melted and cooled	6
1 env. (7 g)	unflavoured gelatin	1 env. (7 g)
¼ cup	lime juice	50 mL
2 tsp	finely grated lime zest	10 mL
1 cup	whipping cream, whipped Strawberries Lime slices	250 mL

◆ Line bottom and sides of an 8½ inch (22 cm) springform pan with ladyfingers, rounded side facing out.

◆ Beat cream cheese and sugar with electric mixer until smooth. Blend in chocolate.

◆ Sprinkle gelatin over lime juice in saucepan. Let stand 5 minutes to soften. Stir mixture over low heat until gelatin is dissolved. Blend warm gelatin and lime peel into cheese mixture.

◆ Fold cheese mixture into whipped cream. Pour into pan. Chill at least 3 hours. Garnish with strawberries and lime slices.

Prep time: 15 minutes plus chilling
Makes 8 to 10 servings.

Pralines 'n Cream Cheesecake

A no-bake masterpiece.

Crust

1 cup	graham crumbs	250 mL
½ cup	finely chopped pecans	125 mL
⅓ cup	butter or margarine, melted	75 mL
¼ cup	packed brown sugar	50 mL

Filling

½ cup	chopped pecans	125 mL
¼ cup	packed brown sugar	50 mL
¼ cup	butter or margarine, melted	50 mL
2 pkgs (250 g each)	PHILADELPHIA BRAND Cream Cheese, softened	2 pkgs (250 g each)
¾ cup	packed brown sugar	175 mL
1 env. (7 g)	unflavoured gelatin	1 env. (7 g)
¼ cup	cold water	50 mL
1 cup	whipping cream, whipped	250 mL
4	squares BAKER'S Semi-Sweet Chocolate, melted and cooled	4

Crust:

◆ Combine crust ingredients. Press onto bottom and 1 inch (2.5 cm) up sides of 8½ inch (22 cm) springform pan.

Filling:

◆ For praline mixture, combine pecans, ¼ cup (50 mL) brown sugar and melted butter, mixing well with fork. Set aside.

◆ Beat cream cheese and remaining sugar with electric mixer until smooth.

◆ Sprinkle gelatin on top of cold water in saucepan. Let stand 5 minutes to soften. Stir mixture over low heat until gelatin is dissolved. Blend warm gelatin into cheese mixture. Fold cheese mixture into whipped cream.

◆ Measure 2 cups (500 mL) of the cheese mixture; fold in chocolate and blend well. Spread all but ½ cup (125 mL) plain cheese mixture into prepared pan.

◆ Sprinkle praline mixture over top. Spread chocolate cheese mixture evenly over praline.

◆ Spoon remaining plain cheese mixture over chocolate mixture and swirl surface with knife to marble. Chill at least 3 hours.

Prep time: 30 minutes plus chilling
Makes 10 to 12 servings.

DOUBLE CHOCOLATE CHEESECAKE

Spectacular layers of white and dark chocolate!

Crust

1 cup	chocolate wafer crumbs	250 mL
3 Tbsp	butter or margarine, melted	45 mL

Filling

3 pkgs (250 g each)	PHILADELPHIA BRAND Cream Cheese, softened*	3 pkgs (250 g each)
¾ cup	sugar	175 mL
3	eggs at room temperature	3
1 tsp	vanilla	5 mL
3	squares BAKER'S White Chocolate, melted and cooled	3
2 Tbsp	raspberry schnapps liqueur (optional)	30 mL
3	squares BAKER'S Semi-Sweet Chocolate, melted and cooled	3

Glaze

¾ cup	whipping cream	175 mL
6	squares BAKER'S Semi-Sweet Chocolate, chopped	6

Crust:

◆ Combine crumbs and butter; press onto bottom of 9 inch (23 cm) springform pan. Bake at 350°F (180°C) for 10 minutes. Cool.

Filling:

◆ Heat oven to 425°F (220°C).

◆ Beat cream cheese and sugar with electric mixer until smooth. Beat in eggs one at a time until just blended. Add vanilla.

◆ Divide batter in half. Stir white chocolate and liqueur into one portion; stir semi-sweet chocolate into remaining portion. Pour dark chocolate batter into pan; spread evenly. Spoon white batter carefully over top; spread evenly.

◆ Bake for 10 minutes; reduce heat to 250°F (120°C). Bake for 30 to 35 minutes longer or until centre of cake is just barely firm.

◆ Remove from oven and run knife around sides of pan. Chill.

Glaze:

◆ Just before serving, bring cream to a simmer over low heat. Add chocolate and stir until melted and smooth. Pour glaze over top of cake. With metal spatula, spread to cover top, allowing some to run over edge to cover sides. Garnish as desired.

Prep time: 20 minutes plus chilling
Baking time: 45 minutes
Makes 10 to 12 servings.

1

Stir white chocolate and liqueur into one half of batter.

2

Stir dark chocolate into remaining half of batter.

3

Pour dark chocolate batter into pan.

4

Spoon white batter carefully over top.

5

Spread glaze over top and sides of cheesecake with metal spatula.

CHOCOLATE RASPBERRY CHEESECAKE

A light chocolate cheesecake!

4	squares BAKER'S Bitter-sweet Chocolate, chopped	4
¼ cup	water	50 mL
1 pkg (250 g)	PHILADELPHIA BRAND Light Cream Cheese Product, softened	1 pkg (250 g)
½ cup	raspberry jam, divided	125 mL
1 cont. (1 L)	COOL WHIP Whipped Topping, thawed, divided	1 cont. (1 L)
2 Tbsp	water	30 mL
36	fresh raspberries	36

◆ Microwave chocolate with ¼ cup (50 mL) water on HIGH for 1 to 1½ minutes or over low heat, stirring constantly until almost melted; remove and stir until completely melted. Mixture will be thick.

◆ Beat chocolate, cream cheese and ¼ cup (50 mL) jam. Immediately stir in 3 cups (750 mL) whipped topping until smooth.

◆ Spread in 8 or 9 inch (20 or 23 cm) pie plate or springform pan. Freeze 3 to 4 hours.

◆ Remove from freezer; let stand 15 minutes. Briefly heat and stir remaining jam and 2 Tbsp (30 mL) water until well blended. Sieve to remove seeds. Garnish with remaining whipped topping, raspberry sauce and raspberries. Store leftover cheesecake in freezer.

Prep time: 20 minutes
Freezing time: 3 to 4 hours
Makes 12 servings.

CHUNKY BITTERSWEET SHORTBREAD

Chocolate and pecan studded shortbread – a new favourite.

2 cups	butter, softened	500 mL
1 cup	fruit or super-fine sugar	250 mL
3½ cups	all-purpose flour	875 mL
½ cup	cornstarch	125 mL
6	squares BAKER'S Bittersweet Chocolate, coarsely chopped	6
1 cup	pecans, toasted, coarsely chopped	250 mL
	Sifted icing sugar	

◆ Heat oven to 350°F (180°C).

◆ Beat butter with sugar until light and fluffy. Mix in flour and cornstarch until well blended. Stir in chocolate and pecans.

◆ Drop by heaping tablespoonfuls onto ungreased cookie sheets, about 1 inch (2.5 cm) apart.

◆ Bake for 20 to 25 minutes or until lightly browned. Cool.

◆ Dust lightly with icing sugar.

Prep time: 20 minutes
Baking time: 25 minutes
Makes 48 cookies.

HOLIDAY NANAIMO BARS

Base

½ cup	butter or margarine, softened	125 mL
3	squares BAKER'S Semi-Sweet Chocolate	3
2 Tbsp	sugar	30 mL
1 tsp	vanilla	5 mL
1	egg	1
2 cups	graham crumbs	500 mL
1 cup	BAKER'S ANGEL FLAKE Coconut	250 mL
½ cup	chopped nuts	125 mL

Filling

2 Tbsp	custard powder	30 mL
3 Tbsp	milk	45 mL
¼ cup	butter or margarine, softened	50 mL
2 cups	sifted icing sugar	500 mL

Icing

5	squares BAKER'S Semi-Sweet Chocolate, chopped	5
1 Tbsp	butter	15 mL

Base:

◆ Melt chocolate with butter in a saucepan. Stir in sugar, vanilla and egg. Remove from heat. Add crumbs, coconut and nuts; mix well. Press into 9 inch (23 cm) square pan. Chill.

Filling:

◆ Beat together all ingredients using electric mixer. Spread over base; chill.

Icing:

◆ Melt chocolate with butter over low heat. Spread over filling. Chill until almost firm. Cut into bars.

***Prep time: 20 minutes plus chilling
Makes about 18 bars.***

Mocha Nanaimo Bars: Follow recipe replacing milk in filling with coffee liqueur blended with 2 tsp (10 mL) instant coffee granules.

Red or Green Nanaimo Bars: Follow recipe adding ½ tsp (2 mL) peppermint extract and a few drops of green or red food colouring to the filling.

Marble Bark

1

Partially melt *each* chocolate over hot water.

2

Remove from heat and continue stirring until melted and smooth.

3

Stir in nuts.

AFTER DINNER CHOCOLATE LIQUEUR CUPS

An after-dinner party treat served with coffee.

2	squares BAKER'S Semi-Sweet Chocolate	2
	Liqueurs (your favourite)	
1 cup	whipping cream, whipped	250 mL

◆ Partially melt chocolate over hot water. Remove from heat and continue stirring until completely melted and smooth.

◆ With a small brush, lightly coat interiors of 16 miniature paper cups with chocolate, making sure entire interior surface of each cup is covered. Freeze for at least 1 hour.

◆ Remove one at a time from freezer. Quickly peel off paper and return to freezer. Store in covered container in freezer until required.

◆ Serve filled with your favourite liqueur and topped with whipped cream.

Prep time: 15 minutes plus chilling
Makes about 16 liqueur cups.

MARBLE BARK

A great holiday gift giving idea.

6	squares *each* BAKER'S Bittersweet and BAKER'S White Chocolate	6
1 cup	whole toasted nuts or dried fruit	250 mL

◆ Chop each square of chocolate into 8 pieces; place into 2 separate small bowls.

◆ Partially melt *each* chocolate over hot water. Remove from heat and continue stirring until melted and smooth.

◆ Stir in half the nuts or dried fruit into *each* bowl of melted chocolate.

◆ Drop spoonfuls of chocolate, alternating white and bittersweet on a waxed paper-lined cookie sheet.

◆ Using the end of a knife, draw the dark and white chocolate together to give a marbled effect. Gently tap cookie sheet on counter to smooth surface. Refrigerate until firm.

Prep time: 15 minutes plus chilling
Break into about 20 pieces.

4

Drop spoonfuls of chocolate onto cookie sheet.

5

Marble chocolate using knife.

RUM BALLS

A quintessential!

2	squares BAKER'S Semi-Sweet Chocolate	2
¼ cup	corn syrup	50 mL
¼ cup	icing sugar, sifted	50 mL
⅓ cup	dark rum	75 mL
2 cups	finely crushed vanilla wafers	500 mL
1 cup	finely chopped pecans	250 mL
	Slightly beaten egg white	
	Chocolate sprinkles or finely chopped pecans	

◆ Melt chocolate over hot water. Add corn syrup, sugar, rum, wafer crumbs and nuts; mix well. Chill until firm enough to handle.

◆ Shape into 1 inch (2.5 cm) balls. Dip in egg white and roll in chocolate sprinkles or chopped pecans. Store in airtight container in refrigerator for at least one week to mellow.

Prep time: 30 minutes plus chilling
Makes about 30 rum balls.

WHITE CHOCOLATE CITRUS BARK

6	squares BAKER'S White Chocolate	6
½ cup each	candied citrus peel and coloured, chopped candied fruit, patted dry	125 mL each

◆ Partially melt chocolate over hot water. Remove from heat and continue stirring until melted and smooth.

◆ Stir in peel and fruit. Spread on waxed paper-lined cookie sheet.

◆ Chill until firm. Break into pieces. Store in refrigerator.

Prep time: 10 minutes plus chilling
Makes about 30 pieces.

CHOCOLATE GLAZED BUTTERBALLS

1¾ cups	all-purpose flour	425 mL
1 cup	finely chopped pecans	250 mL
¾ cup	butter	175 mL
½ cup	icing sugar, sifted	125 mL
¼ tsp	salt	1 mL
¾ tsp	vanilla	3 mL
2 tsp	cold water	10 mL
3	squares BAKER'S Semi-Sweet Chocolate, chopped	3
	Coarsely grated chocolate or finely chopped nuts (optional)	

◆ Heat oven to 325°F (160°C).

◆ Combine flour and pecans; mix well.

◆ Cream butter. Gradually add sugar and continue beating until light and fluffy. Add salt, vanilla and water; blend well. Gradually stir in flour mixture.

◆ Shape into ¾ inch (2 cm) balls. Place on ungreased cookie sheets.

◆ Bake for 20 minutes or until edges just begin to brown. Transfer to rack and cool thoroughly.

◆ Partially melt chocolate over hot water. Remove from heat and continue stirring until completely melted. Dip half of each cookie into melted chocolate. Roll in coarsely grated chocolate or finely chopped nuts, if desired. Place on waxed paper-lined cookie sheet and chill. Store in airtight container.

Prep time: 30 minutes plus chilling
Baking time: 20 minutes
Makes 4 dozen cookies.

FABULOUSLY FLAWLESS FUDGE

8	squares BAKER'S Semi-Sweet Chocolate	8
⅔ cup	sweetened condensed milk	150 mL
1 tsp	vanilla	5 mL
½ cup	chopped nuts (optional)	125 mL

◆ Melt chocolate with milk over low heat. Blend in vanilla; mix well. If desired, add nuts.

◆ Spread in waxed paper-lined 9 × 5 inch (23 × 13 cm) loaf pan. Chill until firm.

Prep time: 10 minutes plus chilling
Makes about 32 pieces.

BITTERSWEET CHOCOLATE TRUFFLES ROYALE

¼ cup	whipping cream	50 mL
6	squares BAKER'S Bittersweet Chocolate, coarsely chopped	6
1 Tbsp	butter, softened	15 mL
2 Tbsp	orange liqueur (optional)	30 mL
6	squares BAKER'S Bittersweet Chocolate, coarsely chopped	6

◆ Bring cream to a boil over medium heat; remove from heat. Add 6 squares of chocolate, butter and liqueur; stir until melted.

◆ Freeze mixture until firm enough to handle, about 1 to 2 hours.

◆ With a teaspoon, form mixture into small balls; freeze 20 minutes.

◆ Partially melt remaining chocolate over hot, not boiling water. Remove from heat and continue stirring until melted and smooth. Dip each ball in chocolate.

◆ Place on waxed paper-lined cookie sheet. Drizzle truffles with remaining melted chocolate. Chill until firm, about 30 minutes

Prep time: 1 hour plus chilling
Makes about 2 dozen truffles.

Bring cream to a boil.

Add chocolate, butter and liqueur and stir until melted.

Form truffle mixture into balls.

Dip balls into partially melted chocolate and place on waxed paper. Drizzle with remaining melted chocolate.

CHOCOLATE FRUITCAKE

A chocolate twist on a classic favourite.

1 cup	candied red cherries, halved	250 mL
1 cup	candied green cherries, halved	250 mL
1 cup	dark or golden raisins	250 mL
½ cup	cut mixed peel	125 mL
¾ cup	dark rum or brandy	175 mL
2 cups	all-purpose flour	500 mL
½ tsp	baking powder	2 mL
½ tsp	salt	2 mL
6	squares BAKER'S Unsweetened Chocolate	6
¾ cup	unsalted butter	175 mL
1⅓ cups	sugar	325 mL
4	eggs	4
½ cup	milk	125 mL
1½ tsp	vanilla	7 mL
1 cup	coarsely chopped blanched almonds	250 mL
	Dark rum or brandy	

◆ Combine cherries, raisins and mixed peel in bowl. Stir in rum. Cover and soak at room temperature for at least a half hour.

◆ Heat oven to 325°F (160°C). Stir flour, baking powder and salt together until evenly blended. Set aside. Melt chocolate over low heat or microwave on MEDIUM power for 3 minutes.

◆ Beat butter and sugar together until creamy. Add eggs, 1 at a time, beating constantly. Beat in milk, vanilla and chocolate. Drain any rum that has not been absorbed by the fruit and beat in.

◆ Gradually beat in dry ingredients. Stir in marinated fruit and nuts. Pour mixture into greased 10 inch (25 cm) tube pan; smooth top.

◆ Bake for 50 to 60 minutes or until toothpick inserted into centre comes out almost clean. Cool in pan on rack. Brush fruitcake with additional rum, then wrap in foil and keep refrigerated or freeze.

Prep time: 20 minutes
Baking time: 60 minutes
Makes 24 servings.

CHOCOLATE DIPPED CHERRIES

2 Tbsp	butter, softened	30 mL
2 Tbsp	corn syrup	30 mL
	Dash of salt	
1 cup	icing sugar, sifted	250 mL
20	maraschino cherries with stems, drained and dried thoroughly	20
5	squares BAKER'S Semi-Sweet Chocolate	5

◆ Combine butter, corn syrup and salt; blend in sugar and mix until smooth. Chill fondant until firm enough to handle.

◆ Wrap about 1 tsp (5 mL) fondant around each cherry to cover completely. Roll between hands to smooth surface. Chill until firm.

◆ Partially melt chocolate over hot water. Remove from heat and continue stirring until melted and smooth.

◆ Dip cherries in chocolate making sure that stem end is completely covered. Place on waxed paper. Chill until chocolate is firm.

◆ Store cherries in refrigerator. Let stand at room temperature for 24 hours before serving, to soften fondant.

Prep time: 1 hour plus chilling
Makes 20 cherries.

Note: Cherries may be soaked in brandy or sherry 24 hours before using. Dry well on paper towel before wrapping in fondant.

TUTTI-FRUTTI BARS

⅓ cup	finely chopped candied pineapple	75 mL
⅓ cup	finely chopped candied cherries	75 mL
⅓ cup	finely chopped candied mixed peel	75 mL
⅓ cup	toasted slivered almonds	75 mL
8	squares BAKER'S Semi-Sweet Chocolate	8

◆ Line bottom of 9 × 5 inch (23 × 13 cm) loaf pan with waxed paper, letting paper extend beyond ends.

◆ Combine fruits and nuts.

◆ Partially melt chocolate over hot water. Remove from heat and continue stirring until melted and smooth.

◆ Pour half of chocolate in bottom of prepared pan. Sprinkle with fruits and nuts. Cover with remaining chocolate. Tap pan several times to settle chocolate. Chill until firm.

◆ Lift chocolate block out of pan, using paper extensions. Remove waxed paper. Cut into bars.

Prep time: 20 minutes plus chilling
Makes about 32 bars.

Florentines

FLORENTINES

A Christmas tradition in the BAKER'S KITCHENS.

1 cup	slivered almonds	250 mL
½ cup	whipping cream	125 mL
½ cup	sugar	125 mL
½ cup	candied peel, diced	125 mL
¼ cup	all-purpose flour	50 mL
8	squares BAKER'S Semi-Sweet Chocolate, chopped	8

◆ Heat oven to 350°F (180°C).

◆ Combine all ingredients except for the chocolate.

◆ Drop teaspoonfuls of mixture 2 inches (5 cm) apart onto greased and floured cookie sheets. Flatten with a knife dipped in water.

◆ Bake for 10 to 12 minutes or until brown around edges. Remove to rack to cool.

◆ Partially melt chocolate over hot water. Remove from heat and continue stirring until melted and smooth. Spread chocolate onto flat side of each cookie. Allow to harden. Store in refrigerator.

Prep time: 60 minutes
Baking time: 12 minutes
Makes about 2 dozen cookies.

CHOCOLATE ALMOND SHORTBREAD

1¼ cups	icing sugar, sifted	300 mL
¾ cup	butter, softened	175 mL
6	squares BAKER'S Semi-Sweet Chocolate, melted and cooled	6
1 tsp	vanilla	5 mL
1 cup	all-purpose flour	250 mL
1 cup	ground almonds	250 mL
¼ tsp	salt	1 mL
1 cup	BAKER'S Semi-Sweet Chocolate Chips	250 mL
½ cup	unblanched coarsely chopped toasted almonds	125 mL

◆ Heat oven to 250°F (120°C).

◆ Cream sugar and butter until light and fluffy. Add chocolate and vanilla; mix well.

◆ Combine flour, ground almonds and salt; mix well. Gradually add to chocolate mixture. Press into a 12 × 9 inch (30 × 23 cm) rectangle on ungreased cookie sheet. Sprinkle evenly with chips and chopped almonds.

◆ Bake for 45 to 50 minutes. Cool; cut into bars.

Prep time: 20 minutes
Baking time: 50 minutes
Makes about 48 bars.

CHOCOLATE PEANUT BUTTER FUDGE

Wrap pieces in coloured cellophane for fancy treats.

6	squares BAKER'S Semi-Sweet Chocolate	6
¼ cup	butter or margarine	50 mL
½ cup	KRAFT Smooth or Crunchy Peanut Butter	125 mL
1 pkg (250 g)	KRAFT Fruit Flavoured or Plain Miniature Marshmallows	1 pkg (250 g)

◆ Melt chocolate and butter over low heat.

◆ Stir in peanut butter; mix well. Fold in marshmallows.

◆ Spread in waxed paper-lined 9 inch (23 cm) square baking pan. Chill until firm, about 2 hours.

◆ Cut into squares. Store in refrigerator.

Prep time: 10 minutes plus chilling
Makes about 3 dozen candies.

◆ *Microwave Directions:* Combine chocolate and butter in large microwaveable bowl. Microwave on MEDIUM power for 3 minutes or until chocolate is melted. Continue as above.

CHOCOLATE PECAN TASSIES

Pastry Shells

1 pkg (250 g)	PHILADELPHIA BRAND Cream Cheese, softened	1 pkg (250 g)	
½ cup	butter or margarine, softened	125 mL	
1½ cups	all-purpose flour	375 mL	

Filling

1	egg	1	
¾ cup	packed brown sugar	175 mL	
1 Tbsp	butter or margarine, melted	15 mL	
1 tsp	vanilla	5 mL	
4	squares BAKER'S Semi-Sweet Chocolate, *each* cut into 12 pieces	4	
1 cup	finely chopped pecans	250 mL	
2	squares BAKER'S Semi-Sweet Chocolate, melted	2	

Pastry Shells:

◆ Beat together cream cheese and butter. Stir in flour.

◆ Gather the dough into a ball, adding more flour if necessary.

◆ Divide the dough into 48 balls. Place each into lightly greased 1¾ inch (4.5 cm) mini tart pans*. Press the dough onto the sides and bottoms. Chill while preparing filling.

Filling:

◆ Heat oven to 350°F (180°C).

◆ Whisk together egg, sugar, butter and vanilla until well blended.

◆ Place one piece of chopped chocolate and 1 tsp (5 mL) of the chopped pecans in the bottom of each shell. Spoon filling evenly into each shell. Sprinkle with remaining pecans.

◆ Bake for 25 to 30 minutes. Cool in pan 30 minutes. Drizzle remaining chocolate on top. Chill.

Prep time: 30 minutes plus chilling
Baking time: 30 minutes
Makes 48.

* These can be made larger if desired.

WHITE CHOCOLATE YULE LOG

Filling

2¼ cups	whipping cream	550 mL
3 *each*	large strips lemon and orange zest	3 *each*
9	squares BAKER'S White Chocolate, coarsely chopped	9

Cake

3	squares BAKER'S White Chocolate	3
2 Tbsp	hot water	30 mL
5	large eggs	5
1 tsp	vanilla	5 mL
½ cup	sugar	125 mL
½ cup	cake and pastry flour	125 mL
1 Tbsp	cornstarch	15 mL
	Icing sugar	

Filling:

◆ Heat cream and zests over medium heat. Remove from heat; let stand 30 minutes. Remove zests; add chocolate. Reheat mixture over medium heat, stirring constantly until melted.

◆ Pour into large bowl; cover tightly. Refrigerate overnight or until mixture is cold and thickened.

Cake:

◆ Heat oven to 350°F (180°C).

◆ Melt chocolate with hot water over low heat.

◆ Beat eggs and vanilla on high speed with electric mixer, gradually adding sugar until mixture is pale and forms thick ribbons when beaters are lifted, about 10 minutes.

◆ Sift flour with cornstarch; gradually fold into egg mixture. Gently fold in chocolate mixture.

◆ Line a greased 15 × 10 inch (40 × 25 cm) jelly roll pan with waxed paper; grease and flour pan. Spread batter into pan; tap gently to remove bubbles.

◆ Bake for 15 to 17 minutes until cake springs back when pressed. Invert immediately onto towel sprinkled generously with icing sugar. Remove paper, trim edges. With narrow end, roll up cake with towel. Cool 30 minutes.

Assembly:

◆ Beat filling on high speed until soft peaks form. Do not overbeat or texture will be grainy.

◆ Unroll cake. Spread half of filling on cake; roll up.

◆ Cut slice on a slant from one end of cake and place next to roll to simulate a branch.

◆ Ice roll with remaining filling. Use tines of a fork to create bark effect. Chill until ready to serve. Freezes well.

Prep time: 45 minutes
Baking time: 17 minutes
Makes 10 servings.

1

Invert cake onto icing sugar covered towel and remove paper.

2

Roll up cake with towel.

3

Spread half of filling on unrolled cake.

4

Roll cake up tightly to form log.

5

Cut slice from cake and place next to roll to simulate branch.

6

Ice roll with remaining filling.

]H[appy Holiday Chocolate Mould

2 cups	strawberry ice cream, softened	500 mL
2 cups	chocolate ice cream, softened	500 mL
½	square BAKER'S Semi-Sweet Chocolate, coarsely chopped	½
¼ cup	slivered almonds, toasted	50 mL
½ cup	candied cherries, halved	125 mL
4	slices pound cake	4
4	squares BAKER'S Semi-Sweet Chocolate, chopped	4
2 Tbsp	butter or margarine	30 mL
1 Tbsp	hot water	15 mL
½	square BAKER'S Semi-Sweet Chocolate, melted	½
	Candied cherries and almonds (optional)	

◆ Press strawberry ice cream firmly into bottom and sides of plastic wrap-lined 4 cup (1 L) bowl.

◆ Combine chocolate ice cream, chopped chocolate, almonds, and cherries; mix well. Spoon into centre of strawberry ice cream shell. Cover ice cream with pound cake slices, trimming where necessary. Cover with plastic wrap. Freeze until firm, at least 4 hours.

◆ Melt 4 squares chocolate with butter over low heat. Gradually add hot water; cool to lukewarm.

◆ Remove mould from freezer. Unmould onto waxed paper and remove plastic wrap. Pour melted chocolate over surface; work quickly with knife to cover evenly. Drizzle with ½ square melted chocolate. Store covered in freezer.

◆ To serve, transfer to serving plate. Garnish with additional candied cherries and almonds.

Prep time: 1 hour plus freezing
Makes about 8 servings.

WHITE CHOCOLATE AND STRAWBERRY TRIFLE

1 pkg (6 serving size)	JELL-O Vanilla Pudding and Pie Filling	1 pkg (6 serving size)
3 cups	milk	750 mL
6	squares BAKER'S White Chocolate, coarsely chopped	6
1 cont. (500 mL)	COOL WHIP Whipped Topping, thawed	1 cont. (500 mL)
½	frozen pound cake, thawed	½
¼ cup	orange liqueur or orange juice	50 mL
2½ cups	sliced and sweetened fresh strawberries	625 mL
5	squares BAKER'S White Chocolate, grated	5
6 – 8	whole strawberries for garnish	6 – 8
1	square BAKER'S White Chocolate, melted and cooled	1

◆ Prepare pudding with milk according to package directions. Remove from heat; stir in 6 squares of chocolate until melted and smooth. Cover with plastic wrap. Chill. Fold in 1 cup (250 mL) whipped topping.

◆ Cut cake into small cubes and drizzle with liqueur.

◆ In the bottom of a deep glass bowl, layer half the cake cubes, half the berries, half the pudding and half the grated chocolate. Repeat layers, ending with chocolate.

◆ Top with remaining whipped topping. Garnish with berries. Drizzle melted chocolate over top.

Prep time: 30 minutes plus chilling
Makes 8 servings.

CHOCOLATE PECAN BARS

This is an ideal recipe for a "cookie exchange"
or gift giving; one pan makes 50 bars!

Crust

3 cups	all-purpose flour	750 mL
½ cup	sugar	125 mL
1 cup	butter, softened	250 mL

Filling

6	squares BAKER'S Semi-Sweet Chocolate, chopped	6
1½ cups	corn syrup	375 mL
1½ cups	sugar	375 mL
4	eggs, slightly beaten	4
1½ tsp	vanilla	7 mL
2¼ cups	chopped pecans	550 mL

Drizzle

2	squares BAKER'S Semi-Sweet Chocolate	2

Crust:

◆ Heat oven to 350°F (180°C).

◆ Beat flour, sugar and butter with electric mixer until mixture resembles coarse crumbs. Press firmly and evenly into greased 15 × 10 inch (40 × 25 cm) jelly roll pan.

◆ Bake for 20 minutes.

Filling:

◆ Place chocolate and corn syrup in saucepan. Over low heat, stir until chocolate melts; remove from heat. Stir in sugar, eggs and vanilla until blended. Stir in pecans.

◆ Pour filling over hot crust; spread evenly.

◆ Bake for 30 minutes or until filling is firm around edges and slightly soft in centre. Cool in pan on rack.

Drizzle:

◆ Melt chocolate over low heat or in microwave on MEDIUM power for 2 to 3 minutes. Drizzle over top.

Prep time: 10 minutes
Cooking time: 50 minutes
Makes about 50 bars.

WHITE CHOCOLATE CRANBERRY CAKE

*White chocolate, citrus and cranberries compliment
this moist pound cake.*

Cake

1 cup	butter	250 mL
1 cup	packed brown sugar	250 mL
½ cup	sugar	125 mL
4	eggs	4
3 Tbsp	orange juice	45 mL
1 Tbsp	orange rind	15 mL
2 cups	all-purpose flour	500 mL
2 tsp	baking powder	10 mL
1½ cups	fresh or frozen cranberries	375 mL
6	squares BAKER'S White Chocolate, chopped	6

Glaze

3	squares BAKER'S White Chocolate, chopped	3
2 Tbsp	orange juice	30 mL
	White chocolate curls	

Cake:

◆ Heat oven to 350°F (180°C).

◆ Grease and flour 9 inch (23 cm) tube or bundt pan.

◆ Beat butter and sugars with electric mixer. Beat in eggs, orange juice and rind. Beat in flour and baking powder. Stir in cranberries and chocolate.

◆ Bake for 60 to 70 minutes or until toothpick inserted in centre comes out clean. Cool in pan for 10 minutes. Turn onto cooling rack. Cool.

Glaze:

◆ Melt white chocolate and orange juice over low heat or in microwave on MEDIUM power 1½ minutes. Stir until smooth.

◆ Drizzle glaze over cake. Garnish with white chocolate curls, or as desired.

Prep time: 20 minutes
Baking time: 70 minutes
Makes 10 to 12 servings.

Note: Freezes well.

WHITE CHOCOLATE
COCONUT LIME TRUFFLES

Coconut Lime Filling

½ cup	whipping cream	125 mL
⅓ cup	canned cream of coconut	75 mL
4 tsp	coarsely grated lime zest	20 mL
12	squares BAKER'S White Chocolate, coarsely chopped	12
2 Tbsp	white or dark rum	30 mL

Coating

10	squares BAKER'S White Chocolate, coarsely chopped	10
2½ cups	BAKER'S ANGEL FLAKE Coconut, toasted	625 mL

Filling:

◆ Bring cream, coconut cream and zest to a boil over medium heat; remove from heat, cover with lid and let stand for 10 minutes. Strain with a sieve into a second saucepan; discard zest.

◆ Reheat until mixture comes to a gentle boil. Add chocolate and rum; stir until melted. Pour into a bowl; cover.

◆ Freeze mixture for about 1 hour. Beat 1 minute with a spoon just until it starts to stiffen.

◆ Freeze another 2 to 3 hours, until mixture is firm enough to handle.

◆ With a teaspoon, roll mixture into small balls; place on cookie sheets. Freeze 1 to 2 hours until firm.

Coating:

◆ Partially melt half of remaining chocolate over hot, not boiling water. Remove from heat and continue stirring until melted and smooth.

◆ Remove half the truffles from freezer. Dip each ball in chocolate then roll in toasted coconut. Place on waxed paper-lined cookie sheet; chill until firm.

Prep time: 60 minutes
Freezing time: 4 to 6 hours
Makes about 4 dozen truffles.

WHITE CHOCOLATE TRUFFLES ROYALE

A white chocolate lovers idea of perfection!

¼ cup	whipping cream	50 mL
6	squares BAKER'S White Chocolate, each cut into 4 pieces	6
1 Tbsp	butter, softened	15 mL
2 Tbsp	orange liqueur (optional)	30 mL
6	squares BAKER'S White Chocolate	6

◆ Bring cream to a boil over medium heat; remove from heat.

◆ Add chocolate, butter and liqueur; stir until melted.

◆ Freeze mixture until firm enough to handle, about 3 to 4 hours.

◆ Form mixture into small balls with a teaspoon; freeze 20 minutes.

◆ Partially melt remaining chocolate over hot, not boiling water. Remove from heat and continue stirring until melted and smooth. Dip each ball in chocolate. Place on waxed paper-lined cookie sheet and chill until firm.

Prep time: 30 minutes
Freezing time: 4 hours
Makes about 1½ dozen truffles.

ICINGS AND SAUCES

CHOCOLATE SATIN SAUCE

This is a very versatile homemade chocolate sauce.

4	squares BAKER'S Semi-Sweet Chocolate, chopped	4
¼ cup	water	50 mL
¼ cup	sugar	50 mL
2 Tbsp	liqueur (orange, almond or coffee) *or*	30 mL
1 Tbsp	vanilla	15 mL
2 Tbsp	butter	30 mL

◆ Melt chocolate with water over low heat; blend until mixture is completely smooth.

◆ Add sugar. Bring to a boil over medium heat and boil 2 minutes, stirring constantly. Remove from heat.

◆ Add liqueur *or* vanilla and butter. Store in refrigerator. Great to have on hand for last minute dessert creations.

Prep time: 15 minutes
Makes about ⅔ cup (150 mL).

Note: Sauce may be reheated over low heat.

CHOCOLATE SYRUP

4	squares Baker's Unsweetened Chocolate, chopped	4
1¼ cups	hot water	300 mL
1 cup	sugar	250 mL
¼ tsp	salt	1 mL
½ tsp	vanilla	2 mL

◆ Melt chocolate with water over low heat; blend until mixture is completely smooth.

◆ Add sugar and salt, bring to a boil, and boil 2 minutes, stirring constantly.

◆ Remove from heat; add vanilla. Cool.

◆ Pour into jar; cover tightly. Keep in refrigerator. Serve over pancakes, waffles or ice cream.

Prep time: 15 minutes
Makes 2 cups (500 mL).

WHITE CHOCOLATE BUTTER ICING

6	squares BAKER'S White Chocolate	6
¼ cup	whipping cream	50 mL
1 cup	cold butter, cut into pieces	250 mL
1 cup	icing sugar, sifted	250 mL

◆ Melt chocolate with cream in a saucepan over very low heat or in microwave on MEDIUM power for 2 minutes, stirring until smooth. Pour into a large bowl; cool to room temperature.

◆ Gradually beat in butter and icing sugar; continue beating until light and fluffy.

Prep time: 15 minutes
Makes about 3 cups (750 mL) icing.

EASY CHOCOLATE ICING

3	squares BAKER'S Unsweetened Chocolate, chopped	3
3 Tbsp	butter	45 mL
3 cups	sifted icing sugar	750 mL
⅛ tsp	salt	0.5 mL
6 Tbsp	milk	90 mL
½ tsp	vanilla	2 mL

◆ Melt chocolate with butter over low heat, stirring constantly.

◆ Combine sugar, salt, milk and vanilla; blend. Add chocolate mixture; mix well.

◆ Let stand, stirring occasionally, until right consistency for spreading. If necessary, chill bowl to thicken.

Prep time: 10 minutes
Makes 1½ cups (375 mL).

Note: Blend in an additional tablespoon (15 mL) of milk if icing becomes too thick for spreading.

MOCHA CHOCOLATE BUTTER ICING

2	squares BAKER'S Unsweetened Chocolate, chopped	2
2 Tbsp	butter	30 mL
¼ cup	hot coffee	50 mL
⅛ tsp	salt	0.5 mL
2 cups	sifted icing sugar	500 mL
1 tsp	vanilla	5 mL

◆ Melt chocolate and butter over hot water; add coffee and salt.

◆ Gradually add icing sugar, then vanilla and beat until smooth.

Prep time: 10 minutes
Makes about 1½ cups (375 mL).

CHOCOLATE CRACKLE SUNDAE

A molten sauce that hardens over ice cream.

2 Tbsp	butter	30 mL
½ cup	chopped pecans	125 mL
4	squares BAKER'S Semi-Sweet Chocolate, chopped	4
	Ice cream	

◆ Melt butter over low heat.

◆ Add nuts; cook, stirring constantly, until light golden brown.

◆ Remove from heat; add chocolate and stir until melted and smooth.

◆ Serve warm over ice cream.

Prep time: 5 minutes
Makes 4 servings.

Hint: Sauce may be made in advance and reheated on top of stove or in microwave oven on MEDIUM power until warm.

ONE-BOWL CHOCOLATE CREAM CHEESE ICING

6	squares BAKER'S Semi-Sweet Chocolate, chopped	6	
3 Tbsp	water	45 mL	
1 pkg (250 g)	PHILADELPHIA BRAND Cream Cheese, softened	1 pkg (250 g)	
1 tsp	vanilla	5 mL	
2½ cups	icing sugar, sifted	625 mL	

◆ Heat chocolate with water in large microwaveable bowl on MEDIUM power 2 to 4 minutes or over low heat, stirring until chocolate is completely melted and smooth. Cool to lukewarm.

◆ Add cream cheese and vanilla; beat until well blended. Gradually beat in icing sugar until well blended and smooth.

Prep time: 15 minutes
Makes about 2½ cups (625 mL) or enough to ice one 13 × 9 inch (33 × 23 cm) cake or two 9 inch (23 cm) layers.

WHITE CHOCOLATE CREAM CHEESE ICING

1 pkg (250 g)	PHILADELPHIA BRAND Cream Cheese, softened	1 pkg (250 g)	
6	squares BAKER'S White Chocolate, melted and cooled	6	
½ cup	butter, softened	125 mL	
1 Tbsp	milk*	15 mL	

* Substitute with 1 Tbsp (15 mL) liqueur or rum

◆ Beat cream cheese until fluffy. Gradually beat in chocolate, butter and milk until well blended.

Prep time: 15 minutes
Makes 2 cups (500 mL).

Note: Make sure chocolate is completely cooled before adding to cream cheese.

INDEX